MECO®

BARBECUE&SMOKER COOKBOOK

Produced by *MarketLink Custom Publishing*, 2100 Lakeshore Drive,
Birmingham, Alabama 35209

Copyright 1993 by Oxmoor House, Inc.
Book Division of Southern Progress Corporation
P.O. Box 2463, Birmingham, Alabama 35201

Recipes adapted from *Southern Living*® cookbooks. *Southern Living* is a
federally registered trademark belonging to Southern Living, Inc.

Library of Congress Catalog Number: 93-083174
ISBN: 0-8487-1229-3

Manufactured in the United States of America
Third Printing 1994

Editor-in-Chief: Nancy J. Fitzpatrick
Senior Foods Editor: Susan Carlisle Payne
Senior Editor, Editorial Services: Olivia Kindig Wells
Director of Manufacturing: Jerry R. Higdon
Art Director: James Boone

MECO Barbecue & Smoker Cookbook

Editor: Julie Fisher
Copy Editor: Donna Baldone
Editorial Assistant: Kelly E. Hooper
Designer: Alison T. Bachofer
Illustrator: Caroline Wellesley
Production Manager: Rick L. Litton
Associate Production Manager: Theresa L. Beste
Production Assistant: Marianne Jordan
Cover Photographer: Ralph Anderson
Cover Photo Stylist: Virginia R. Cravens

Cover: Texas-Style Game Hens (page 35), Marinated Pork Tenderloins (page 29),
Herbed Potatoes on the Grill (page 51), Marinated Beef Kabobs (page 15).

The MECO® grills featured in the introduction portion of the cookbook are available at retail
stores throughout the U.S. and Canada. For information on ordering additional copies of
the *MECO Barbecue & Smoker Cookbook*, or for the name of the MECO dealer nearest you,
simply call 1-800-346-3256. Or write to: MECO Corporation,
1500 Industrial Road, Greeneville, TN 37743.

CONTENTS

Contents

INTRODUCTION

Barbecuing has come a long way since the days when the Spaniards arrived on the south Atlantic Coast to find the Indians cooking meat and fish on green wood racks over open fires or hot stones. This process was called boucan.

The Spanish renamed it barbacoa, which eventually became barbecue. Still later, other early inhabitants of the New World liked the smoked flavor so much that they made barbecuing a part of their social life.

In the 1700s, the outdoor barbecue became the favorite gathering theme for New York society, while at the same time, politicians adopted it as a rallying point for electioneering.

Over the years, various barbecue cooking methods have evolved regionally. From state to state, across the country, mopping and sopping sauces differ in color and intensity, ranging from deep tomato-red to transparent sneaky-hot.

Meat preferences vary from region to region, too. In the Deep South pork is popular, while Texas and Oklahoma prefer beef. In western Kentucky, mutton shares the honors with pork. Chicken emerges on top in eastern Tennessee, but pork is not far behind. If you travel far enough West, cabrito (goat meat) is the favorite. And in between, fish and seafood are gaining in popularity.

TYPES OF MECO GRILLS

MECO offers a wide selection of barbecue grills and accessories, ranging from lightweight foldup charcoal braziers to deluxe electric cart grills and water smokers.

When buying a grill, consider these points: where you might grill and how often, what kind of food you like to cook, and the number of people you usually serve.

Following are some specifics on the different types of MECO grills to assist you in selecting the right one for your needs.

BRAZIERS: A brazier is a French term for a pan that holds burning coals. Of the two charcoal brazier models that are offered, one has a 380-square-inch cooking grid that snap-locks into a shallow bowl. It also has folding legs for easy portability and storage.

The other model features a 214-square-inch cooking grid in a shallow bowl on three legs. This is an ideal tabletop or picnic grill.

SMOKER GRILLS: MECO offers several charcoal smoker grills, from fixed leg models to those with wheels and pedestal bases. All models feature an adjustable 21½-inch-square grid with tilt-away hoods, adjustable air vents in the hood and bowl, and 350 square inches of cooking area. Some models come with foldaway side tables, a leg shelf, and an elevated fire grate and ash dump.

These grills are great for cooking large amounts of food. In addition, they impart a unique smoked flavor to food when used with the hood closed.

ELECTRIC GRILLS: A large selection of patented electric grills is available, ranging from small tabletop models to deluxe cart models on wheels. All are listed by Underwriters Laboratories and operate on 120-volt household current.

These grills are very convenient and easy to use. They are ready to cook in five to ten minutes and offer a variable heat control that can sear a steak on high or slow cook a slab of ribs on medium setting. Cooking grid sizes range from 176 to 215 square inches. All models feature a tiltaway hood, adjustable air vents, and a grease collection cup. Some models have adjustable heating element positions, a hood window, a porcelain-coated grid, and a rotisserie feature.

WATER SMOKERS: These grills come in charcoal and electric models, with single or double cooking levels. All models have 380-square-inch cooking grids and porcelain-coated water pans. Some models have heat indicators and sliding access doors for adding water and charcoal. The charcoal models can be used to smoke, roast, grill, or steam food and can cook up to six hours using a single pan of charcoal. The electric models cook with constant, even heat and can be used to smoke or steam food. Water smokers are ideal for turkey, chicken, roast, ham, ribs, and fish. The double grid models can cook up to 50 pounds of meat at once.

LOCK & GO PORTABLE GRILLS: This is the ideal grill for camping or picnicking. It is available in both a charcoal and an electric model. Both models feature a 214-square-inch cooking grid, adjustable air vents, and an interlocking hood and bowl. The charcoal model has an internal charcoal pan for both direct and indirect cooking and easy cleaning. The electric model has a removable thermostat heat control, a heat reflector pan for more efficient cooking, and a UL Approved 1650-watt heating element. The Lock & Go portable grill can be used as a brazier or a smoker grill.

BARBECUING SAFETY

All manufacturers of barbecue grills provide specific instruction manuals and directions for proper use. Please read and follow these instructions carefully because failure to do so may result in property damage, serious personal injury, or death.

• Never use charcoal or gas grills for indoor cooking. Toxic carbon monoxide fumes can accumulate and cause death.
• Never use gasoline, kerosene, or alcohol for igniting charcoal. These fuels may explode or flash when igniting, resulting in serious burns.
• Always keep children and pets away from a hot grill.
• Do not place a hot grill on a combustible surface.
• After cooking, make sure the coals are cold before disposal.

FOOD PREPARATION TIPS

• Wash hands thoroughly with hot soapy water before and after handling food.
• Defrost frozen meats completely in the refrigerator or microwave oven.
• Use a timer to remind you when to check or turn food on the grill.

• Prevent food from sticking by coating the cooking grid with cooking oil or vegetable cooking spray prior to grilling.

• Transfer cooked foods from grill to table using clean utensils and plates.

• Add salt to meat after grilling is complete. Salt tends to extract the natural juices from meat during cooking.

• Use sugar or tomato-based sauces only during the last 15 to 20 minutes of direct grilling to prevent burning or charring.

• Always use tongs for turning meat. Piercing meat with a fork causes it to lose natural juices.

• Use a meat thermometer to check the doneness of meat near the end of the recommended cooking time. Insert it into the thickest area, being careful not to touch bone or fat.

• Remove meat from the grill when the internal temperature registers the desired doneness, and let it stand 15 minutes before carving. (While the meat stands, it may continue to cook slightly.)

BUILDING A CHARCOAL FIRE

Use a high quality hardwood charcoal to make the hottest, longest-lasting fire. Line the bottom of the fire bowl with heavy-duty aluminum foil.

For grills not equipped with an elevated charcoal pan or grate, spread a one-inch layer of sand or small gravel over bottom. This will allow the charcoal to burn better and protect the bottom of the grill. Place enough charcoal in the grill to extend about one inch beyond the food to be cooked. Place the charcoal in a pyramid-shaped stack in the center of the grill.

Pour charcoal lighter fluid evenly over the charcoal and let it soak in for one minute. Carefully light the charcoal, and let it burn 30 to 45 minutes or until the coals are mostly covered in white ash.

The temperature ranges for coals are as follows: low coals, under 300°; medium coals, 300° to 350°; medium-hot coals, 350° to 400°; hot coals, 400° to 500°.

MARINATING MEATS

Marinades are used to tenderize meats and enhance their flavor. They lubricate and moisten the surface of meat to prevent it from becoming dry over the hot coals. Use about one-half cup of marinade for every pound of meat.

Choose glass or plastic containers or heavy-duty, zip-top plastic bags in which to marinate meats. Avoid metal containers. Refrigerate items in marinades as follows: beef, pork, lamb, and poultry—2 to 8 hours or overnight; fish—1 to 4 hours.

CHARCOAL GRILL COOKING

Cooking with a charcoal fire may be done with either an open brazier grill or a covered smoker grill using one of the methods below. Grilling on an open brazier or a covered grill with the hood open should be done with the coals arranged for the Direct Method. Grilling on a covered smoker grill with the hood closed may be done with the Direct Method for smokier flavor in foods that cook in less than 25 minutes.

The Indirect Method should be used for meats that require longer than 25 minutes to cook. To begin, fully open all grill vents, build the fire, and arrange the coals for the intended cooking method. Use long-handled tongs and a grill mitt to arrange coals. Keep a timer and water-mist bottle handy for extinguishing flare-ups.

DIRECT METHOD

This method is best for grilling hamburgers, hot dogs, steaks, chops, and chicken pieces. When the coals are ready, spread them evenly in a single layer. For the hottest fire, arrange the coals so all are touching. For less heat, spread them apart. For grills with adjustable cooking grid levels, arrange the coals with about ½-inch space between them for even heat distribution. Then adjust the grid level closer or farther away from the coals to get the desired heat for the food you are cooking.

INDIRECT METHOD

This method is best for foods that require more than 25 minutes of cooking time, such as roasts, whole poultry, and hams. This method should be done in a covered grill with the hood closed for uniform heat. Use a drip pan under the meat that extends about one inch beyond the meat. This drip pan may be purchased or made from a double thickness of heavy-duty aluminum foil. To begin, build a fire with about 40 charcoal briquettes. When ready, pile half the coals along the front of the fire bowl and half along the back, leaving space in the center of the bowl for the drip pan. Place the drip pan in the center. Now place the meat on the cooking grid over the drip pan and close the hood. If your grill has adjustable air vents, you can better control the cooking temperature inside. With the vents fully open, the grill will cook food faster because the temperature of the coals will be hotter. The more the grill is closed, the slower it will cook the food, providing a smokier flavor. With vents fully closed, the coals will go out.

ELECTRIC GRILL COOKING

The MECO electric grill is a recent advancement in outdoor cooking. It uses a patented energy-efficient concept of infrared reflectivity that has the grill ready to cook in ten minutes. It can sear a steak in minutes or slow-cook chicken in an hour. The grilled taste is produced by the meat juices falling on the heating element and reflector pan, which creates the smoke that flavors the meat; this is done without the use of charcoal or lava rock. The control knob and a pilot light let you know when the heating element is energized. Cooking times are basically the same as when cooking with charcoal.

SMOKER COOKING

Smoker cooking is a process of cooking over a low smoky fire for a long period of time. Meats that have been cooked this way have a distinct smoky flavor and are very tender and moist. For most smoke cooking, a pan of hot water is placed between the heat source and the cooking grid. The water simmers, adds moisture to the smoke, and keeps the heat lower. Soaked wood pieces are added to the hot charcoal or placed on the electric heating element as needed to produce the smoke.

For best results, add green or dampened wood pieces to the hot coals, electric heating element, or lava rock. Hardwoods, mesquite, and fruit woods are the best woods to use. Hickory and oak add a robust flavor. Mesquite imparts a milder taste. All three are good with beef, pork, shellfish, fish, and poultry. Fruit woods such as apple and cherry add a light smoked flavor and go well with poultry. Alder has a delicate aroma and complements fish, especially trout and salmon. Do not use cedar, fir, pine, spruce, or any other woods with evergreen needle leaves. The resin in these woods gives food an unpleasant bitter taste.

Soak dry wood chips in water at least 30 minutes; soak larger chunks for several hours. This will cause the wood to smoke longer instead of burning up too quickly. For foods which cook in 30 minutes or less, use chips. For meats that require a longer cooking time, use chunks.

Just before putting the meat on the grill, scatter the wood evenly over the hot coals or on the electric element and wait a few minutes for it to begin smoking. Then add the food to the grill. For a smokier flavor, add more wood as the food cooks.

Another way to cook in a charcoal smoker is to dry-smoke or roast in it. This method adds a delicious flavor to meat when the fat and juices drip onto the hot charcoal and smoke. To do this, remove the water pan and place the meat on the cooking grid in its highest position above the charcoal and smoking wood. Cooking times are generally shorter using this method since the water pan is not there blocking the heat. Some of the best Southern pork barbecue is made by cooking a 20-pound whole pork shoulder for

12 to 14 hours using this method and hickory wood for smoking.

Long, slow smoker cooking is quite a variation from today's hurried life-style, but the results are worth the extra time it takes. It also takes some scheduling of your time. Base your schedule on the average cooking time for a recipe and count backward from the time you want to eat. Then add one hour for starting the fire, removing the meat from the refrigerator to get the chill off, and preparing everything to cook. This first hour of preparation is the most work that you'll have to do.

To get started, place the smoker outdoors on a level surface that won't burn and away from open windows and doors. For a charcoal smoker, build the fire in the fire pan in the bottom of the smoker using at least five pounds of good quality hardwood charcoal. When cooking very large cuts of meat requiring longer cooking times, start with ten pounds of charcoal. Allow the charcoal to burn until covered in white ash, about 30 to 45 minutes. For an electric smoker, plug it in and preheat about ten minutes.

Place two or three soaked wood chunks directly on the hot charcoal or electric heating element. Using heavy gloves or mitts, place the water pan in position above the charcoal or element. Fill the pan with hot tap water and any other ingredients called for in your recipe. Put the cooking grid in place, and arrange the food in a single layer on the grid. Always leave a little space between each piece of food so the smoke and heat can circulate evenly. Place the cover on the smoker and begin cooking. Do not lift the cover again until the end of the minimum cooking time unless it is necessary to add water or charcoal.

If you are cooking longer than four hours, you may have to add more water to the drip pan. A full pan of charcoal should last about six hours. Add more wood chunks as needed for a smokier flavor.

At the end of the minimum cooking time, insert a meat thermometer into the thickest part of the meat, making sure it doesn't touch bone or fat. When done, remove the meat to a platter, and let it stand about 15 minutes before carving.

For successful smoker cooking, thaw food prior to cooking. If additional charcoal is required, be sure it is hot and covered with white ash prior to adding it to the smoker. To do this, you will need to start it in a separate grill or some other metal container at least 30 minutes before it's needed.

Additional cooking time may be required if it's windy, colder than 60°, or if you lift the cover frequently.

Do not use "instant lighting" charcoal. It burns with too much flame and for too long a time to use in a smoker. This can damage the paint, delay your cooking, and may cause the food to absorb the petroleum fumes and acquire a bad taste.

BEEF

BARBECUED CHUCK ROAST

1 (3- to 4-pound) boneless chuck roast
(2 to 3 inches thick)
4 cloves garlic, minced
¼ cup olive oil
1 teaspoon dried rosemary
2 teaspoons soy sauce
½ teaspoon dry mustard
¼ cup red wine vinegar
¼ cup sherry (optional)
2 tablespoons catsup
1½ teaspoons commercial steak sauce
½ teaspoon Worcestershire sauce

Place roast in a large shallow container. Sauté garlic in olive oil in a small skillet; add rosemary, soy sauce, and dry mustard, stirring well. Remove from heat, and stir in red wine vinegar and, if desired, sherry; pour over roast. Cover and marinate in refrigerator 6 to 8 hours, turning roast occasionally.

Remove roast from marinade, reserving marinade. Add catsup, steak sauce, and Worcestershire sauce to marinade, stirring well; baste roast with sauce. Insert meat thermometer into thickest part of roast, making sure it does not touch fat. Grill, covered, over hot coals 40 minutes or until thermometer registers 140° (rare), 160° (medium), or 170° (well done). Turn roast, and baste frequently with sauce. Let stand 15 minutes before slicing. Yield: 6 to 8 servings.

BARBECUED RIB ROAST

2 tablespoons lemon-pepper seasoning,
divided
1 (6- to 8-pound) boneless beef rib roast
Marinade
Mesquite or oak chunks
Savory Barbecue Sauce
Additional lemon-pepper seasoning

Rub 1 tablespoon lemon-pepper seasoning over surface of roast. Place roast in a large shallow container. Set aside 2 cups marinade for use in Savory Barbecue Sauce; pour remaining marinade over roast. Cover and marinate in refrigerator 6 hours, turning roast occasionally.

Soak mesquite chunks in water to cover for several hours. Drain and set aside.

Remove roast from marinade, discarding marinade. Rub remaining 1 tablespoon lemon-pepper seasoning over surface of roast. Insert meat thermometer into thickest part of roast, making sure it does not touch fat. Set roast aside.

Prepare charcoal fire in grill; let burn 30 to 45 minutes or until coals are white. Rake coals to one end of grill; place wood chunks on hot coals. Place roast at opposite end; cover with lid.

Grill, covered, over indirect heat 2½ to 3 hours or until thermometer registers 140° (rare), 160° (medium), or 170° (well done). Baste every hour with Savory Barbecue Sauce. Sprinkle roast with additional lemon-pepper seasoning. Let roast stand 15 minutes before slicing. Yield: 12 to 16 servings.

Marinade:
3½ cups water
1½ cups Burgundy or other dry
red wine
¾ cup red wine vinegar
1 small onion, sliced
1 stalk celery, chopped
1 clove garlic, crushed

Combine all ingredients, stirring marinade well. Yield: 6 cups.

Savory Barbecue Sauce:
2 cups reserved marinade
2 cups beer
1 cup vegetable oil
¼ cup plus 2 tablespoons herb-pepper
seasoning

Combine all ingredients, stirring sauce well. Yield: 5 cups.

MARINATED BEEF ROAST ON THE ROTISSERIE

1 (5- to 6-pound) beef tenderloin,
   trimmed
3½ cups Magnificent Marinade (see
   page 45)

Place tenderloin in a large shallow dish or a heavy-duty, zip-top plastic bag; pour Magnificent Marinade over tenderloin. Cover and marinate in refrigerator 6 to 8 hours, turning occasionally.

Remove tenderloin from marinade, discarding marinade. Tie tenderloin securely with heavy string at 2-inch intervals. Thread tenderloin on spit; secure with prongs at each end of spit. Balance tenderloin properly to avoid strain on motor. Place spit on rotisserie 4 to 6 inches from heating element. Grill tenderloin, covered, on medium-hot setting of electric grill 1½ to 2 hours or until meat thermometer registers 140° (rare) or 160° (medium). Remove tenderloin from spit. Let stand 15 minutes before slicing. Yield: 10 to 12 servings.

NOTE: When using a charcoal grill, grill, covered, over medium-hot coals, using indirect method with a drip pan.

DENTON, TEXAS, BARBECUED BEEF BRISKET

1 (4- to 6-pound) beef brisket, trimmed
¾ cup red wine vinegar
½ cup firmly packed brown sugar
½ cup pineapple juice
⅓ cup molasses
⅓ cup prepared mustard
1 tablespoon minced onion
3 tablespoons Worcestershire sauce
1 teaspoon chili powder
¼ teaspoon hot sauce

Place brisket in a large heavy-duty, zip-top plastic bag. Combine vinegar and remaining ingredients, stirring well; pour over brisket, and secure bag tightly. Turn bag to coat brisket thoroughly. Place bag in a shallow container; marinate in refrigerator 4 to 8 hours, turning bag occasionally.

Remove brisket from marinade, reserving marinade. Prepare charcoal fire in grill. Grill brisket over medium coals until browned. Cover with lid, and grill 15 minutes. Turn brisket, and baste with reserved marinade; set remaining marinade aside. Cover and grill brisket an additional 15 minutes.

Wrap brisket in heavy-duty aluminum foil, allowing room for marinade. Cut a hole in top of foil; pour remaining marinade through hole over brisket. Press foil together to seal hole. Cover and continue to grill over medium coals 1½ to 2 hours or until very tender. To serve, diagonally slice brisket across grain into thin slices. Yield: 12 to 16 servings.

GRILLED BRISKET WITH PANHANDLE BARBECUE SAUCE

1 (4- to 5-pound) beef brisket, trimmed
1 tablespoon garlic salt
1½ teaspoons coarsely ground pepper
Panhandle Barbecue Sauce

Sprinkle brisket with garlic salt and pepper. Wrap brisket in heavy-duty aluminum foil. Prepare fire in grill. Place brisket on grill. Cover with lid, and open vent. Grill over low coals 2 hours or until very tender.

To serve, diagonally slice brisket across grain into thin slices. Serve with Panhandle Barbecue Sauce. Yield: 12 to 14 servings.

Panhandle Barbecue Sauce:
2 (14-ounce) bottles catsup
1 cup firmly packed brown sugar
½ cup butter or margarine
3 tablespoons lemon juice
2 tablespoons liquid smoke
2 tablespoons Worcestershire sauce

Combine all ingredients in a large saucepan, stirring well; bring mixture to a boil. Reduce heat, and simmer sauce, uncovered, 25 to 30 minutes, stirring occasionally. Yield: 3½ cups.

TOURNEDOS DIABLES

1 (5- to 7-pound) beef tenderloin, trimmed
Garlic salt to taste
Coarsely ground pepper to taste
1 (6-ounce) package long grain and wild rice
2 cups beef bouillon
⅓ cup sherry
¼ cup cognac
2 teaspoons butter or margarine
1 tablespoon plus 1 teaspoon Dijon mustard
1 tablespoon tomato paste
1 teaspoon Worcestershire sauce
½ teaspoon garlic powder
½ teaspoon white vinegar
1 cup sliced fresh mushrooms
1 cup chopped green onions

Sprinkle tenderloin with garlic salt and pepper. Insert meat thermometer into tenderloin, making sure it does not touch fat. Grill tenderloin over medium coals 15 minutes on each side or until thermometer registers 140° (rare) or 160° (medium). Set aside, and keep warm.

Prepare rice according to package directions. Set aside, and keep warm.

Place bouillon in a medium saucepan, and bring to a boil. Reduce heat, and simmer bouillon, uncovered, while completing recipe.

Combine sherry and cognac in a small, long-handled saucepan; heat just until warm (do not boil). Remove from heat.

Immediately ignite sherry mixture with a long match, and pour over bouillon. When flames die down, stir in butter, Dijon mustard, tomato paste, Worcestershire sauce, garlic powder, and vinegar. Cook, uncovered, over low heat 15 minutes. Stir in mushrooms and green onions; cook an additional 5 minutes. Remove sauce from heat.

Cut tenderloin into ½-inch slices. Place rice on a serving platter; top with meat and sauce. Yield: 10 to 14 servings.

MARINATED BARBECUED CHUCK STEAK

1 (2-pound) chuck steak (about 1 inch thick)
⅓ cup lemon juice
¼ cup olive oil
2 tablespoons minced onion
1 clove garlic, minced
1 tablespoon chili powder
1 teaspoon salt
2 teaspoons ground ginger

Trim excess fat from steak, and place steak in a large shallow container. Combine lemon juice and remaining ingredients, stirring well; pour marinade mixture over steak. Cover and marinate in refrigerator 6 to 8 hours, turning steak occasionally.

Remove steak from marinade, discarding marinade. Grill over hot coals 8 to 10 minutes on each side or until desired degree of doneness. Yield: 2 servings.

MARINATED STEAK CUBES

2 (8- to 12-ounce) T-bone or rib-eye steaks (1 inch thick)
1½ cups Magnificent Marinade (see page 45)
Hickory chunks

Place steaks in a large heavy-duty, zip-top plastic bag. Pour marinade over steaks. Seal bag securely. Marinate in refrigerator 5 to 6 hours, turning steaks occasionally.

Soak hickory chunks in water to cover for at least 1 hour. Prepare charcoal fire in grill; let burn 30 to 45 minutes or until coals are white. Place hickory chunks on coals. Remove steaks from marinade; discard marinade. Place steaks on grill, and close grill hood. Cook 5 to 6 minutes on each side or to desired degree of doneness.

To serve, cut steaks into 1-inch cubes; insert a wooden pick into each cube, and arrange on a serving tray. Yield: 6 to 8 appetizer servings.

GRILLED BLACK PEPPER STEAK

2 (1½- to 2-pound) sirloin steaks (1½ to 2 inches thick)
2 large onions, thinly sliced
2 cloves garlic, minced
2 cups red wine vinegar
1 cup vegetable oil
⅔ cup firmly packed brown sugar
½ teaspoon salt
½ teaspoon dried marjoram
½ teaspoon dried rosemary
6 drops of hot sauce
2 tablespoons plus 2 teaspoons coarsely ground pepper, divided

Place steaks in a large shallow container. Combine sliced onion and next 8 ingredients, stirring well; pour over steaks. Cover and marinate in refrigerator 3 hours, turning steaks occasionally.

Remove steaks from marinade. Press 2 teaspoons pepper into each side of each steak. Grill steaks over hot coals 15 minutes on each side or until desired degree of doneness. Yield: 6 servings.

TANGY FLANK STEAK

1 (1- to 1½-pound) flank steak
½ cup vegetable oil
1 tablespoon plus 1½ teaspoons chopped fresh parsley
3 tablespoons white vinegar
3 tablespoons lemon juice
2 tablespoons Worcestershire sauce
2 tablespoons soy sauce
1½ teaspoons salt
2 teaspoons dry mustard
1 teaspoon freshly ground pepper
½ teaspoon garlic salt

Place steak in a shallow container. Combine oil and remaining ingredients, stirring well; pour over steak. Cover and marinate in refrigerator 2 hours, turning steak often.

Remove steak from marinade. Grill over hot coals 10 to 12 minutes on each side or until desired degree of doneness. To serve, diagonally slice steak across grain into thin slices. Yield: 4 to 6 servings.

FLANK STEAK PINWHEELS

2 (1- to 1½-pound) flank steaks
2 cups chopped onion
4 cloves garlic, minced
1 cup vegetable oil
⅔ cup white vinegar
2 teaspoons salt
½ teaspoon dried thyme
½ teaspoon dried marjoram
Dash of pepper

Diagonally slice steaks across grain into ¼-inch-thick slices; roll up slices, and secure with wooden picks. Place pinwheels in a 13- x 9- x 2-inch baking dish; sprinkle with onion. Combine garlic and remaining ingredients, stirring well; pour marinade over pinwheels. Cover and marinate in refrigerator 6 hours.

Remove pinwheels from marinade. Grill over medium-hot coals 14 to 16 minutes or until desired degree of doneness, turning pinwheels frequently. Yield: 8 to 10 servings.

FAVORITE FAJITAS

1 pound flank or skirt steak
Juice of 2 to 3 limes
1 to 1½ teaspoons garlic salt
½ teaspoon pepper
4 (8-inch) flour tortillas
Vegetable toppings or sauce (optional)

Place steak in a large heavy-duty, zip-top plastic bag. Combine lime juice, garlic salt, and pepper; pour over steak, and secure bag. Place bag in a large shallow container; marinate in refrigerator 6 to 8 hours, turning bag occasionally.

Wrap tortillas in aluminum foil, and bake at 325° for 15 minutes or until heated. While tortillas bake, remove steak from marinade. Grill over medium-hot mesquite coals 5 to 6 minutes on each side or until desired degree of doneness.

Diagonally slice steak across grain into thin slices. Wrap warm tortillas around steak, and top with any of the following ingredients, if desired: chopped tomato, green onions, guacamole, sour cream, picante sauce, or taco sauce. Yield: 4 servings.

BARBECUED BEEF SHORT RIBS

1 tablespoon butter or margarine
⅓ cup chopped onion
1 tablespoon plus 1 teaspoon all-purpose flour
1 cup apple cider or apple juice
3 tablespoons sweet pickle relish
1 tablespoon catsup
¼ teaspoon salt
¼ teaspoon dried basil
⅛ teaspoon ground allspice
Dash of ground cloves
4 pounds beef short ribs

Melt butter in a medium saucepan over low heat; add chopped onion, and sauté until onion is tender. Add flour, stirring well. Cook 1 minute, stirring constantly. Gradually add apple cider, and cook over medium heat, stirring constantly, until mixture thickens. Stir in remaining ingredients except ribs. Remove sauce from heat, and set aside.

Cut ribs into serving-size portions, and grill over low coals 1 hour and 10 minutes. Baste ribs with sauce, and grill an additional 20 minutes or until desired degree of doneness. Turn and baste frequently with sauce.

Bring any remaining sauce to a boil in a saucepan. Remove from heat, and serve with ribs. Yield: 4 servings.

SMOKED BEEF ROAST

1 (4- to 6-pound) beef tenderloin, top round roast, or other boneless beef roast, trimmed
Magnificent Marinade (see page 45)
Hickory, mesquite, or oak chunks

Place tenderloin in a large heavy-duty, zip-top plastic bag. Pour Magnificent Marinade over tenderloin. Seal bag securely. Marinate in refrigerator 8 hours, turning occasionally.

Soak wood chunks in water to cover for several hours.

Prepare charcoal fire by piling charcoal in one end of grill; let burn 30 to 45 minutes or until coals are white. Arrange coals around outer edge of grill. Place a drip pan in center of coals. Place soaked wood chunks on coals.

Remove tenderloin from marinade, reserving marinade. Place tenderloin on rack directly over drip pan. Insert meat thermometer into thickest portion of tenderloin. Cover and cook 3 to 4 hours or until thermometer registers 140° (rare), 150° (medium rare), or 160° (medium). Baste roast with reserved marinade every 2 hours. Add more charcoal as needed. Yield: 10 to 12 servings.

BEEF KABOBS DELUXE

2 pounds boneless sirloin tip roast, cut into 2-inch cubes
½ cup vegetable oil
¼ cup soy sauce
¼ cup white vinegar
½ teaspoon pepper
6 to 8 boiling onions
½ pound fresh mushrooms
1 cup cherry tomatoes
1 large green pepper, cut into 1-inch pieces

Place meat cubes in a large heavy-duty, zip-top plastic bag. Combine oil, soy sauce, vinegar, and pepper, stirring well; pour marinade over meat. Seal bag securely. Cover and marinate in refrigerator 4 to 8 hours, turning bag occasionally.

Parboil onions 3 to 5 minutes. Drain.

Remove meat from marinade, reserving marinade. Alternate meat and vegetables on skewers. Grill kabobs over medium coals 5 minutes on each side or until desired degree of doneness. Baste frequently with marinade. Yield: 6 to 8 servings.

SKEWERED STEAK WITH VEGETABLES

2 pounds boneless sirloin steak
½ cup Chablis or other dry white wine
½ cup vegetable oil
2 tablespoons chili sauce
1 tablespoon white vinegar
1 teaspoon Worcestershire sauce
½ teaspoon salt
½ teaspoon dried oregano
½ teaspoon dried thyme
1 clove garlic, crushed
½ pound fresh mushroom caps
2 large green peppers, cut into 1½-inch pieces
1 pint cherry tomatoes
4 small yellow squash, cut into 1-inch-thick slices

Trim excess fat from steak; cut steak into 1-inch cubes. Place meat cubes in a large shallow container. Combine wine, oil, chili sauce, vinegar, Worcestershire sauce, salt, oregano, thyme, and garlic, stirring well; pour over meat. Cover and marinate in refrigerator 2 to 8 hours; stir occasionally.

Remove meat from marinade, reserving marinade. Alternate meat and vegetables on skewers. Grill kabobs over medium coals 15 minutes or until desired degree of doneness. Turn and baste frequently with marinade. Yield: 6 to 8 servings.

MARINATED BEEF KABOBS

1 pound boneless sirloin steak
1 (8-ounce) bottle Russian salad dressing
2 tablespoons lemon juice
1 tablespoon Worcestershire sauce
⅛ teaspoon garlic powder
⅛ teaspoon pepper
About 10 slices bacon, cut in half
2 medium-size green peppers, cut into 1-inch pieces
1 large onion, cut into 2-inch pieces
½ pound fresh mushrooms
1 pint cherry tomatoes

Trim excess fat from steak; cut into 1½-inch cubes. Place meat cubes in a shallow container. Combine dressing and next 4 ingredients, stirring well; pour over meat. Cover and marinate in refrigerator 6 to 8 hours, stirring meat occasionally.

Remove meat from marinade, reserving marinade. Wrap bacon around meat cubes; secure with wooden picks. Alternate meat and vegetables on skewers. Grill kabobs over medium-hot coals 10 minutes or until desired degree of doneness. Turn and baste frequently with marinade. Yield: 4 servings.

POOR BOY FILLETS

1 pound ground beef
1 (4-ounce) can mushroom stems and pieces, drained
¼ cup grated Parmesan cheese
3 tablespoons finely chopped pimiento-stuffed olives
2 tablespoons finely chopped green pepper
2 tablespoons finely chopped onion
½ teaspoon salt
½ teaspoon lemon-pepper seasoning
6 slices bacon

Shape ground beef into a 12- x 7½-inch rectangle on wax paper. Combine mushrooms and next 6 ingredients, stirring well; sprinkle evenly over beef.

Starting at short end, roll up jellyroll fashion, lifting wax paper to support ground beef while rolling. Carefully slide beef roll onto a baking sheet, seam side down. Smooth and shape beef roll, using your hands. Cover and refrigerate roll 2 to 3 hours.

Cook bacon until limp but not brown. Drain. Cut beef roll into 6 (1½-inch-thick) slices. Wrap a slice of bacon around edge of each fillet; secure with wooden picks. Grill fillets over hot coals 8 minutes on each side or until desired degree of doneness. Yield: 6 servings.

SEASONED BURGERS

1 pound ground chuck
2 tablespoons chopped green
   pepper
1 tablespoon dried onion flakes
1 tablespoon prepared horseradish
2 teaspoons Worcestershire sauce
2 teaspoons prepared mustard
½ teaspoon chili powder
¼ teaspoon salt
⅛ teaspoon pepper
Lettuce leaves
4 hamburger buns
4 slices process American cheese

Combine first 9 ingredients, stirring until combined. Shape mixture into 4 patties.

Grill over medium coals 4 to 5 minutes on each side or until desired degree of doneness. Place lettuce on bottom half of each bun; top with a meat patty and cheese slice. Cover with top of bun, and serve. Yield: 4 servings.

STUFFED HAMBURGERS

2 tablespoons butter or margarine
1¼ cups herb-seasoned stuffing mix
1 (4-ounce) can chopped mushrooms,
   drained
1 egg, beaten
⅓ cup beef broth
¼ cup sliced green onions
¼ cup chopped almonds, toasted
1 teaspoon lemon juice
3 pounds ground beef
1 teaspoon salt
Lettuce leaves
8 hamburger buns
8 slices process American cheese

Melt butter in a medium saucepan over low heat; remove from heat. Stir in stuffing mix and next 6 ingredients. Set stuffing mixture aside.

Combine ground beef and salt, stirring until combined. Shape into 16 patties. Top 8 patties with ¼ cup stuffing mixture on each. Cover with remaining patties, pinching edges to seal. Place patties in a lightly greased wire grilling basket. Grill over medium coals 10 to 12 minutes on each side or until desired degree of doneness. Place lettuce on bottom half of each bun; top with a meat patty and cheese slice. Cover with top of bun, and serve. Yield: 8 servings.

FRANKFURTERS WITH CONDIMENTS

12 beef frankfurters
12 frankfurter buns
Prepared mustard
Mayonnaise
Catsup
1 cup sweet pickle relish
1 medium onion, chopped
1 (8-ounce) package sharp Cheddar
   cheese, shredded
1 (15½-ounce) can chili without beans
   (optional)

Grill frankfurters over hot coals, turning frequently, until browned.

Spread cut sides of buns with desired amounts of mustard, mayonnaise, and catsup. Add frankfurters; top with pickle relish, onion, and cheese. Heat chili thoroughly, and spoon over frankfurters, if desired. Yield: 12 servings.

FISH & SHELLFISH

GRILLED STRIPED BASS

6 (¾-inch-thick) striped bass steaks (about 2 pounds)
½ cup butter or margarine, melted
⅓ cup sherry
⅓ cup lemon juice
1 clove garlic, minced
3 tablespoons soy sauce
2 tablespoons chopped fresh dill
1 teaspoon salt
2 tablespoons butter or margarine, melted

Rinse fish thoroughly in cold water; pat dry, and place in a large shallow container. Combine ½ cup melted butter and next 6 ingredients, stirring well; pour over fish. Cover and marinate in refrigerator 30 minutes, turning fish once.

Remove fish from marinade, reserving marinade. Grill over hot coals 10 minutes on each side or until fish flakes easily when tested with a fork. Baste frequently with marinade. Remove to a serving platter, and pour 2 tablespoons melted butter evenly over fish. Yield: 6 servings.

BARBECUED BASS

8 freshwater bass fillets (4 ounces each)
1 teaspoon salt
¼ teaspoon pepper
¼ teaspoon paprika
8 slices bacon, divided
1 tablespoon plus 1 teaspoon lemon juice, divided

Rinse fillets thoroughly in cold water; pat dry, and sprinkle with salt, pepper, and paprika. Set fillets aside.

Place 2 slices bacon on a large piece of heavy-duty aluminum foil; place a bass fillet lengthwise on each bacon slice. Sprinkle ½ teaspoon lemon juice over each fillet. Fold foil edges over, and wrap securely. Repeat

procedure with remaining ingredients to make 3 additional packets.

Grill packets over hot coals 10 minutes. Turn packets, and grill an additional 10 minutes or until fish flakes easily when tested with a fork. Yield: 4 servings.

GRILLED BLUEFISH

6 bluefish fillets (about 8 ounces each)
1 cup commercial barbecue sauce (or see Sauce chapter)

Rinse fillets thoroughly in cold water; pat dry, and place in a lightly greased wire grilling basket. Grill over hot coals 3 to 5 minutes on each side or until fish flakes easily when tested with a fork. Baste frequently with sauce. Yield: 6 servings.

SMOKED CATFISH

7 pounds catfish, cut into 1½-inch-thick steaks (with skin on)
2 cups water
½ cup firmly packed brown sugar
¼ cup salt
2 tablespoons concentrated liquid crab and shrimp boil
¼ teaspoon dried dillweed
Hickory chunks

Place catfish in a large shallow dish. Combine remaining ingredients except wood chunks; pour over fish. Cover; marinate in refrigerator 1 to 4 hours, turning occasionally. Soak wood chunks in water several hours.

Prepare charcoal fire in smoker, and let burn 30 to 45 minutes. Cover coals with hickory chunks. Place water pan in smoker. Add hot water to fill pan.

Place lower food rack on appropriate shelf in smoker. Arrange catfish on food rack. Cover with smoker lid, and cook 3 to 4 hours. Yield: 12 servings.

GRILLED GROUPER

½ cup olive oil
1 tablespoon plus 1½ teaspoons grated
  Parmesan cheese
1 tablespoon minced onion
2 teaspoons salt
¾ teaspoon sugar
¾ teaspoon dry mustard
¾ teaspoon pepper
¾ teaspoon dried basil
¾ teaspoon dried oregano
¼ cup red wine vinegar
1 tablespoon lemon juice
1 (2-pound) grouper fillet

Combine olive oil, Parmesan cheese, onion, salt, sugar, mustard, pepper, basil, and oregano in container of an electric blender; cover and process 30 seconds. Add vinegar and lemon juice; process an additional 30 seconds. Set olive oil mixture aside.

Rinse fillet thoroughly in cold water; pat dry. Place fillet in a lightly greased wire grilling basket.

Grill over hot coals 10 minutes on each side or until fish flakes easily when tested with a fork. Baste frequently with olive oil mixture. Yield: 6 servings.

GRILLED KING MACKEREL

1½ pounds king mackerel fillets
8 slices white bread
¼ cup plus 2 tablespoons butter or
  margarine, softened
2 tablespoons lemon juice

Rinse fillets thoroughly in cold water; pat dry. Grill over hot coals 10 minutes on each side or until fish flakes easily when tested with a fork. Remove from grill; keep warm.

Lightly toast bread on both sides. Combine butter and lemon juice; beat at medium speed of an electric mixer until smooth. Spread mixture over hot toast; cut toast in half, and top with fish. Yield: 4 servings.

LEMON-GRILLED ORANGE ROUGHY

4 orange roughy fillets (about 4 ounces
  each)
1 tablespoon butter or margarine, melted
½ teaspoon dried thyme
½ teaspoon grated lemon rind
2 tablespoons lemon juice
¼ teaspoon salt
¼ teaspoon paprika
Dash of garlic powder

Rinse fillets thoroughly in cold water; pat dry. Combine butter and remaining ingredients, stirring well; baste fillets with lemon mixture. Grill over hot coals 5 minutes on each side or until fish flakes easily when tested with a fork. Yield: 4 servings.

GRILLED SALMON STEAKS

½ cup butter or margarine, melted
Juice of 1 lemon
½ teaspoon salt
¼ teaspoon ground white pepper
4 (1-inch-thick) salmon steaks (about 1½
  pounds)
1½ teaspoons chopped fresh dill

Combine butter, lemon juice, salt, and pepper, stirring well. Set butter mixture aside.

Rinse fish thoroughly in cold water; pat dry, and place in a lightly greased wire grilling basket. Grill over medium coals 10 minutes on each side or until fish flakes easily when tested with a fork. Baste frequently with half of butter mixture. Add dill to remaining butter mixture, stirring well. Serve fish with dill-butter sauce. Yield: 4 servings.

GRILLED SHARK

6 (½-inch-thick) shark steaks (about 1½ pounds)
¼ cup plus 2 tablespoons commercial Italian salad dressing
¼ cup water
1½ teaspoons dried basil
1½ teaspoons chopped fresh parsley
1½ teaspoons lemon juice
1½ teaspoons dry sherry
⅛ teaspoon garlic powder

Rinse fish thoroughly in cold water; pat dry. Combine dressing and remaining ingredients, stirring well; baste fish with dressing mixture. Set remaining mixture aside.

Place fish in a well-greased wire grilling basket. Grill over medium coals 6 to 8 minutes on each side or until fish flakes easily when tested with a fork. Baste often with remaining dressing mixture. Yield: 6 servings.

GRILLED SWORDFISH

6 (1-inch-thick) swordfish steaks (about 2 pounds)
½ cup vegetable oil
¼ cup lemon juice
2 teaspoons salt
½ teaspoon Worcestershire sauce
¼ teaspoon white pepper
Dash of hot sauce
⅛ teaspoon paprika, divided

Rinse fish thoroughly in cold water; pat dry. Combine vegetable oil and next 5 ingredients, stirring well; baste fish with lemon juice mixture, and sprinkle with half of paprika. Set remaining lemon juice mixture and paprika aside.

Place fish in a greased wire grilling basket. Grill over medium coals 8 minutes on each side or until fish flakes easily when tested with a fork. Baste frequently with remaining lemon juice mixture, and sprinkle with remaining paprika. Yield: 6 servings.

MARINATED GRILLED TROUT

6 dressed freshwater trout, butterflied (about 12 ounces each)
Marinade
1 tablespoon chopped fresh chives
6 fresh thyme sprigs
6 lemon wedges

Rinse fish thoroughly in cold water; pat dry, and place in a large shallow container. Pour marinade over fish. Cover and marinate in refrigerator 1 to 4 hours, turning fish once.

Remove fish from marinade, reserving marinade. Open butterflied fillets, and place skin side down on grill. Sprinkle with chives, and top each fillet with a sprig of thyme. Lightly squeeze juice from lemon wedges over fish; place one lemon wedge on top of each fillet.

Grill butterflied fillets over medium coals 10 minutes or until fish flakes easily when tested with a fork. Baste frequently with marinade. Yield: 6 servings.

Marinade:
1 cup vegetable oil
1 tablespoon plus 1 teaspoon salt
2 tablespoons grated Parmesan cheese
1½ teaspoons sugar
1½ teaspoons Worcestershire sauce
½ cup white vinegar
2 tablespoons lemon juice

Combine first 5 ingredients in container of an electric blender; process 30 seconds. Add vinegar and lemon juice; process an additional 30 seconds. Cover and refrigerate marinade until ready to use. Yield: 1½ cups.

CEDARVALE GARDENS TROUT IDA

6 dressed freshwater trout, butterflied (about 12 ounces each)
1 (16-ounce) bottle commercial Italian salad dressing

Rinse fish thoroughly in cold water; pat dry, and place in a large shallow container. Pour dressing over fish. Cover and marinate in refrigerator 1 to 4 hours, turning fish once.

Remove fish from marinade. Grill, skin side down, over hot coals 10 minutes or until fish flakes easily when tested with a fork. Yield: 6 servings.

SMOKED TROUT

7 pounds trout, cut into 1½-inch-thick steaks (with skin on)
2 cups water
½ cup firmly packed brown sugar
¼ cup salt
¼ teaspoon ground red pepper
Hickory chunks

Place fish in a large dish. Combine water, sugar, salt, and pepper; pour over fish. Cover; marinate in refrigerator 1 to 4 hours, turning often. Soak wood chunks in water 2 hours.

Prepare charcoal fire in smoker, and let burn 30 to 45 minutes. Cover coals with hickory chunks. Place water pan in smoker. Add hot water to fill pan.

Arrange trout on upper food rack on appropriate shelf in smoker. Cover with smoker lid, and cook 3 to 4 hours or until desired degree of doneness. Yield: 12 servings.

GRILLED TUNA STEAKS

12 (1-inch-thick) tuna steaks (about 6 pounds)
1 cup lemon juice
½ cup soy sauce
2 bay leaves
½ teaspoon dried thyme

Rinse fish thoroughly in cold water; pat dry, and place in a large shallow container.

Combine lemon juice, soy sauce, bay leaves, and thyme, stirring well; pour mixture over fish. Cover and marinate in refrigerator 1 hour, turning fish frequently.

Remove fish from marinade, reserving marinade. Place fish in 2 well-greased wire grilling baskets. Grill over hot coals 20 minutes or until fish flakes easily when tested with a fork. Turn and baste occasionally with marinade. Yield: 12 servings.

SCALLOP-BACON KABOBS

1 pound fresh or frozen scallops, thawed
1 small pineapple, cut into 1-inch pieces
18 fresh mushroom caps
3 medium-size green peppers, cut into 1-inch pieces
18 cherry tomatoes
¼ cup vegetable oil
¼ cup lemon juice
¼ cup Chablis or other dry white wine
¼ cup soy sauce
2 tablespoons chopped fresh parsley
½ teaspoon salt
½ teaspoon pepper
¼ teaspoon garlic powder
12 slices bacon, cut in half

Place scallops, pineapple, and vegetables in a large shallow container. Combine oil and next 7 ingredients, stirring well; pour over mixture in container. Cover and marinate in refrigerator 1 to 1½ hours, stirring often. Cook bacon until limp but not brown. Drain and set aside.

Remove scallops, pineapple, and vegetables from marinade, reserving marinade. Alternate with bacon on skewers. Grill kabobs over hot coals 10 to 12 minutes or until bacon is crisp. Turn and baste frequently with marinade. Yield: 6 servings.

MARINATED AND GRILLED SHRIMP

2 pounds unpeeled, large fresh
  shrimp
⅓ cup sherry
⅓ cup sesame oil
⅓ cup soy sauce
½ teaspoon sugar
¼ teaspoon garlic powder
¼ teaspoon ground ginger

Peel and devein shrimp; place in a shallow container. Combine sherry and remaining ingredients; stir well.

Pour sherry mixture over shrimp. Cover and marinate in refrigerator 2 to 3 hours, stirring shrimp occasionally.

Remove shrimp from marinade, reserving marinade. Thread shrimp on skewers.

Grill over medium-hot coals 3 to 4 minutes on each side or until desired degree of doneness. Baste frequently with marinade. Yield: 6 servings.

MESQUITE SHRIMP

1 cup Mesquite chips
2 pounds unpeeled, large fresh or frozen
  shrimp, thawed
Herb Butter Sauce (see page 45)

Soak 8 (12-inch) wooden skewers and wood chips in water for 30 minutes; set aside. Peel shrimp, leaving tails intact, and devein. Thread shrimp evenly onto skewers.

Place soaked wood chips directly onto hot coals or heating element of an electric grill. Grease food rack; place over coals or heating element. Place skewers on rack when wood is smoking, and baste shrimp with Herb Butter Sauce.

Grill, covered, over medium coals or medium setting 3 to 4 minutes. Turn and baste with remaining Herb Butter Sauce. Cover and cook an additional 3 minutes or until shrimp turn pink. Yield: 6 servings.

PARTY BARBECUED SHRIMP

2 pounds unpeeled, large fresh shrimp
½ cup vegetable oil
½ cup lemon juice
¼ cup soy sauce
3 tablespoons finely chopped parsley
2 tablespoons finely chopped onion
1 clove garlic, crushed
½ teaspoon salt
½ teaspoon pepper

Peel and devein shrimp, and place in a large shallow container. Combine oil and remaining ingredients, stirring well; pour over shrimp. Cover and marinate in refrigerator 2 to 3 hours, stirring shrimp occasionally.

Remove shrimp from marinade, and thread on skewers. Grill skewered shrimp over medium coals 3 to 4 minutes on each side or until desired degree of doneness. Remove shrimp to a serving platter. Serve shrimp on wooden picks. Yield: 12 appetizer servings.

GRILLED LOBSTER TAILS

¼ cup plus 2 tablespoons butter, melted
2 tablespoons lemon juice
½ teaspoon salt
⅛ teaspoon pepper
⅛ teaspoon dried tarragon
6 frozen lobster tails, thawed

Combine all ingredients except lobster tails, stirring well. Set sauce aside.

Split lobster tails lengthwise, cutting through upper shell and meat to, but not through, bottom shell. Press shell halves apart to expose meat; baste with sauce.

Place lobster tails, shell side down, on grill. Grill over medium coals 20 minutes. Turn lobster, and grill an additional 5 minutes or until desired degree of doneness.

Bring any remaining sauce to a boil in a saucepan. Serve lobster with remaining sauce. Yield: 6 servings.

SMOKEHOUSE OYSTERS

Hickory chips
Rock salt
1 dozen oysters on the half shell, drained
⅛ teaspoon salt
⅛ teaspoon pepper
¼ cup butter or margarine, softened
**2 tablespoons finely chopped green
    onions**
**2 tablespoons finely chopped fresh
    parsley**
3 tablespoons corn flake crumbs
3 tablespoons grated Parmesan cheese

Soak hickory chips in water to cover for 30 minutes. Drain and set aside.

Sprinkle a thin layer of rock salt in a 13- x 9- x 2-inch baking pan lined with heavy-duty aluminum foil. Arrange oysters (in shells) over rock salt; sprinkle oysters with salt and pepper.

Combine softened butter, green onions, and parsley, stirring well; dot each oyster with butter mixture. Combine corn flake crumbs and Parmesan cheese, stirring well; sprinkle over oysters. Set oysters aside.

Prepare charcoal fire in grill; let burn 30 to 45 minutes or until coals are white. Place wood chips over hot coals. Place pan of oysters on grill, and cover grill with lid. Grill over hot coals 20 minutes or until crumbs are browned and oyster edges curl. Yield: 4 appetizer servings.

NOTE: Rock salt is used to hold shells upright and keep oysters hot.

GRILLED SOFT-SHELL CRABS

1 cup vegetable oil
2 tablespoons white vinegar
1 teaspoon salt
1 teaspoon lemon-pepper seasoning
1 teaspoon lemon juice
¼ teaspoon dried tarragon
⅛ teaspoon garlic powder
12 dressed soft-shell crabs

Combine all ingredients except crabs, stirring until blended. Cover and refrigerate sauce at least 8 hours.

Position crabs securely, back side down, in a wire grilling basket. Grill over hot coals 10 minutes, basting frequently with sauce.

Turn crabs, and grill an additional 5 minutes or until desired degree of doneness. Baste frequently with remaining sauce. Yield: 6 servings.

LAMB

OVEN-BARBECUED LEG OF LAMB

1 (8½- to 9-pound) leg of lamb
1 clove garlic, sliced
⅔ cup all-purpose flour
1 teaspoon salt
1 teaspoon ground ginger
1 teaspoon dry mustard
½ teaspoon pepper
2 tablespoons chili sauce
2 tablespoons olive oil
1 tablespoon Worcestershire sauce
1 tablespoon white vinegar
2 medium onions, sliced
1 cup boiling water

Trim excess fat from leg of lamb. Using a sharp knife, cut several small slits on outside of lamb; stuff with garlic slices.

Combine flour, salt, ginger, dry mustard, and pepper, stirring well; rub mixture over surface of lamb. Set lamb aside.

Combine chili sauce, oil, Worcestershire sauce, and vinegar, stirring until blended. Set sauce aside.

Place lamb, fat side up, in a large roasting pan. Insert meat thermometer into lamb, making sure it does not touch bone or fat. Arrange onion slices around lamb in pan. Baste lamb with sauce.

Bake, uncovered, at 400° for 25 minutes. Reduce heat to 350°, and bake an additional 1 hour and 15 minutes or until thermometer registers 140° (rare) or 160° (medium). Baste lamb every 15 minutes with sauce. Add boiling water to roasting pan during last hour of baking time.

Remove lamb and onion slices to a serving platter, discarding pan drippings. Let stand 15 minutes before slicing.

Bring remaining sauce to a boil in a saucepan. Remove from heat, and serve with lamb. Yield: 12 servings.

GRILLED LEG OF LAMB

Hickory chunks
1 (7- to 8-pound) leg of lamb
15 cloves garlic, sliced
1 teaspoon salt
½ teaspoon pepper
½ teaspoon dried oregano

Soak hickory chunks in water to cover for several hours. Drain and set aside.

Trim excess fat from leg of lamb. Using a sharp knife, cut several small slits on outside of lamb; stuff with garlic slices. Rub salt, pepper, and oregano over surface of lamb. Wrap lamb in heavy-duty aluminum foil. Insert meat thermometer through foil into lamb, making an opening so that thermometer does not touch foil, bone, or fat.

Prepare charcoal fire in grill; let burn 30 to 45 minutes. Place wood chunks on hot coals. Place leg of lamb on grill; cover with lid, and open vent. Grill over medium coals 2 hours or until thermometer registers 140° (rare) or 160° (medium). Let stand 15 minutes before slicing. Yield: 10 servings.

GRILLED LAMB CHOPS

4 (1-inch-thick) lamb rib chops
2 tablespoons butter or margarine, softened
1½ teaspoons chopped fresh parsley
½ teaspoon salt
Dash of pepper
Dash of paprika
1 teaspoon lemon juice

Trim excess fat from chops. Combine butter, parsley, salt, pepper, and paprika; stir well. Stir in lemon juice. Spread butter mixture over chops. Grill chops over medium coals 5 to 6 minutes on each side or until desired degree of doneness. Yield: 4 servings.

TERIYAKI LAMB CHOPS

6 (1-inch-thick) lamb sirloin chops
½ cup finely chopped onion
2 cloves garlic, sliced
¼ cup soy sauce
¼ cup cider vinegar
2 tablespoons honey
2 teaspoons ground ginger
¼ teaspoon dry mustard
¼ teaspoon pepper

Trim excess fat from chops, and place chops in a large shallow container. Combine remaining ingredients, stirring well; pour over chops. Cover and marinate in refrigerator 6 to 8 hours, turning chops occasionally.

Remove chops from marinade, reserving marinade. Grill over medium coals 8 to 10 minutes on each side or until desired degree of doneness. Baste frequently with marinade. Yield: 6 servings.

LAMB CHOPS WITH BÉARNAISE SAUCE

4 (1-inch-thick) lamb sirloin chops
2 tablespoons soy sauce
1 tablespoon catsup
1 tablespoon vegetable oil
½ teaspoon coarsely ground pepper
1 clove garlic, minced
Béarnaise Sauce

Trim excess fat from chops, and place chops in a large shallow container. Combine soy sauce, catsup, oil, pepper, and garlic, stirring well; baste chops with soy sauce mixture. Cover and marinate in refrigerator 6 to 8 hours.

Grill chops over medium coals 5 to 8 minutes on each side or until desired degree of doneness. Serve with Béarnaise Sauce. Yield: 4 servings.

Béarnaise Sauce:
3 tablespoons white wine vinegar
2 teaspoons minced shallots
½ teaspoon dried tarragon
3 egg yolks
⅛ teaspoon salt
⅛ teaspoon ground red pepper
2 tablespoons lemon juice
½ cup butter or margarine

Combine vinegar and shallots in a small saucepan; bring to a boil over medium heat. Reduce heat, and simmer until half of liquid evaporates. Strain, reserving liquid; discard solids. Let vinegar mixture cool slightly; stir in tarragon. Set aside.

Beat egg yolks, salt, and red pepper in top of a double boiler; gradually add lemon juice, stirring constantly. Add one-third of butter to egg mixture; cook over hot (not boiling) water, stirring constantly, until butter melts.

Add another third of butter, stirring constantly. As sauce thickens, stir in remaining butter; cook until sauce is thickened. Remove from heat immediately. Add vinegar mixture to sauce, stirring well. Serve immediately. Yield: ¾ cup.

BARBECUED LAMB CHOPS

8 (2-inch-thick) lamb rib chops
Salt and pepper to taste
3 cloves garlic, halved
½ cup red wine vinegar
¼ cup vegetable oil
Pinch of dried rosemary

Trim excess fat from lamb chops, and sprinkle chops with salt and pepper. Rub garlic over surface of chops. Combine red wine vinegar, vegetable oil, and rosemary, stirring well; baste chops with vinegar mixture. Set remaining vinegar mixture aside.

Grill chops over medium coals 12 minutes on each side or until desired degree of doneness. Baste frequently with vinegar mixture. Yield: 8 servings.

OVEN-BARBECUED LAMB SHANKS

2 to 2½ pounds lamb shanks
½ cup all-purpose flour
¼ cup shortening, melted
1 teaspoon salt
¼ teaspoon pepper
1 cup water
1 medium onion, finely chopped
½ cup raisins
½ cup white vinegar
¼ cup catsup
8 pitted prunes
2 tablespoons brown sugar
2 tablespoons Worcestershire sauce

Dredge lamb shanks in flour, coating well. Sauté lamb in shortening in a large skillet over medium heat until browned. Drain on paper towels. Place lamb in a lightly greased 2½-quart shallow baking dish; sprinkle with salt and pepper.

Combine water and remaining ingredients, stirring well; pour over lamb. Cover and bake at 300° for 2 hours or until lamb is tender. Yield: 4 servings.

LAMB KABOBS

1½ pounds boneless lamb, cut into
   1-inch cubes
¼ cup plus 2 tablespoons white wine
   vinegar
¼ cup plus 2 tablespoons water
2 tablespoons chopped fresh parsley
1 tablespoon plus 1½ teaspoons sugar
1 tablespoon dried rosemary
2 tablespoons dry sherry
½ teaspoon salt
¼ teaspoon pepper
6 large fresh mushroom caps

Place lamb cubes in a large shallow container. Combine vinegar and next 7 ingredients, stirring well; pour marinade over lamb. Cover and marinate in refrigerator at least 2 hours, stirring lamb occasionally.

Remove lamb from marinade, reserving marinade. Place ½ cup marinade in a small saucepan; set aside.

Reserve remaining marinade for basting. Thread lamb on 6 skewers. Grill over medium coals 15 to 20 minutes or until desired degree of doneness. Turn and baste frequently with reserved marinade.

Add mushroom caps to marinade in saucepan; bring to a boil. Reduce heat, and simmer, uncovered, 4 to 5 minutes. Drain. Thread a mushroom cap onto each skewer. Yield: 6 servings.

SHISH KABOBS TERIYAKI

1 pound boneless lamb, cut into 1-inch
   cubes
¼ cup soy sauce
¼ cup white vinegar
¼ cup vegetable oil
1 clove garlic, minced
¼ teaspoon ground ginger
4 cherry tomatoes
1 medium-size green pepper, cut into
   1-inch pieces
1 (8-ounce) can pineapple chunks,
   drained
1 (8-ounce) can whole water chestnuts,
   drained

Place lamb cubes in a large shallow container. Combine soy sauce, vinegar, oil, garlic, and ginger, stirring well; pour over lamb. Cover and marinate in refrigerator 6 to 8 hours, stirring lamb occasionally.

Remove lamb from marinade, reserving marinade. Alternate lamb, tomatoes, green pepper, pineapple, and water chestnuts on skewers.

Grill over medium coals 10 minutes on each side or until desired degree of doneness. Baste kabobs frequently with marinade. Yield: 4 servings.

SHISH KABOBS

2 pounds boneless lamb, cut into
  1½-inch cubes
½ cup diced onion
1 small clove garlic, minced
½ cup olive oil
¼ cup Burgundy or other dry red wine
½ teaspoon salt
½ teaspoon dried oregano
⅛ teaspoon freshly ground pepper
Dash of red pepper
1 medium onion, cut into 1-inch pieces
1 medium-size green pepper, cut into
  1-inch pieces
8 cherry tomatoes

Place lamb cubes in a large shallow container. Combine diced onion and next 7 ingredients, stirring mixture well; pour over lamb cubes. Cover and marinate in refrigerator 6 to 8 hours, stirring lamb occasionally.

Remove lamb from marinade, reserving marinade. Alternate lamb and vegetables on skewers. Grill kabobs over medium coals 15 to 20 minutes or until desired degree of doneness. Turn and baste frequently with marinade. Yield: 8 servings.

OVERNIGHT SHISH KABOBS

2 pounds boneless lamb, cut into 1-inch
  cubes
1 onion, finely diced
½ cup Burgundy or other dry red wine
⅓ cup finely diced green pepper
¼ cup olive oil
½ teaspoon pepper
¼ teaspoon rubbed sage
⅛ teaspoon dry mustard
⅛ teaspoon dried oregano

Place lamb in a large shallow container. Combine onion, wine, diced green pepper, oil, pepper, sage, mustard, and oregano, stirring well; pour over lamb. Cover and marinate in refrigerator 6 to 8 hours or overnight, stirring lamb occasionally.

Remove lamb from marinade mixture, reserving marinade. Thread lamb on skewers, and grill over medium coals 15 to 20 minutes or until desired degree of doneness. Turn and baste frequently with marinade. Yield: 6 to 8 servings.

PORK

HICKORY-SMOKED BARBECUE PORK ROAST

Hickory chunks
2 tablespoons coarsely ground pepper
1 (4-pound) Boston butt pork roast
½ pound pork fat, cut into 1-inch-thick strips
1 cup Vinegar Basting Sauce (see page 44)
1 cup Memphis-Style Barbecue Sauce (see page 44)

Soak hickory chunks in water to cover for several hours.

Rub pepper on roast. Prepare charcoal fire by piling charcoal in one end of grill; let burn 30 to 45 minutes or until coals are white. Arrange coals around outer edge of grill. Place a drip pan in center of coals. Place soaked hickory chunks on coals.

Place pork fat over each pile of coals. Place roast on rack directly over drip pan. Insert meat thermometer into center of roast. Cover and cook over medium coals 5 to 7 hours or until thermometer registers 170°. Turn pork fat and roast, and baste roast with Vinegar Basting Sauce every hour. Add more charcoal and wood chunks as needed.

Let roast stand 15 minutes. Coarsely chop meat, and serve with Memphis-Style Barbecue Sauce. Yield: 8 to 10 servings.

BARBECUED LEG OF PORK

1 (14- to 16-pound) leg of pork
Fiery Barbecue Sauce

Prepare charcoal fire in grill; let burn 30 to 45 minutes or until coals are white. Insert meat thermometer into leg of pork, making sure it does not touch bone or fat.

Place pork on grill. Cover and cook over low coals 4½ hours; turn pork occasionally. Baste with Fiery Barbecue Sauce. Add more charcoal as needed. Cover and cook 2 hours

or until thermometer registers 160° (medium). Baste frequently with Fiery Barbecue Sauce. Let stand 15 minutes before slicing. Serve with reserved 2 cups sauce. Yield: 20 to 25 servings.

Fiery Barbecue Sauce:
1 cup water
¾ cup firmly packed brown sugar
¾ cup catsup
½ cup white vinegar
½ cup Worcestershire sauce
½ cup butter or margarine
¼ cup lemon juice
1 tablespoon salt
1 tablespoon plus 1 teaspoon dry mustard
1 tablespoon plus 1 teaspoon chili powder
1 tablespoon plus 1 teaspoon paprika
2 teaspoons ground red pepper

Combine all ingredients in a large saucepan; stir well. Cook, uncovered, over medium heat until sugar dissolves, stirring frequently. Set aside 2 cups sauce for serving, and use remainder for basting. Yield: about 4 cups.

SLICED BARBECUED PORK

4 cups catsup
2 cups white vinegar
2 tablespoons plus ¼ teaspoon lemon
   juice
1 tablespoon hot sauce
1½ teaspoons Worcestershire sauce
½ teaspoon olive oil
½ teaspoon prepared mustard
¼ teaspoon garlic salt
½ cup cider vinegar
¾ teaspoon hot sauce
1 (5- to 5½-pound) pork shoulder roast

Combine first 8 ingredients in a small Dutch oven, stirring well. Cook, uncovered, over low heat 1 hour, stirring occasionally. Remove sauce from heat. Set sauce aside.

Combine cider vinegar and ¾ teaspoon hot sauce, stirring well. Set vinegar mixture aside. Insert meat thermometer into thickest part of roast, making sure it does not touch bone or fat.

Grill roast over low coals 6 to 7 hours or until thermometer registers 170° (well done). Turn and baste frequently with vinegar mixture. Baste roast with sauce during last hour of grilling time. Let stand 15 minutes before slicing.

Bring remaining sauce to a boil in a saucepan. Remove from heat. Slice pork roast thinly, and toss with enough sauce to coat well. If desired, cover and refrigerate remaining sauce for later use. Yield: 8 servings.

LOUISIANA-STYLE SPIT-ROASTED PORK

1 (6½- to 7-pound) boneless pork loin
   roast, rolled and tied
1 cup soy sauce
1 cup Burgundy or other dry red wine
½ cup cider vinegar
¼ cup lemon juice
½ teaspoon prepared mustard
3 cloves garlic, minced

Place pork roast in a heavy-duty, zip-top plastic bag. Combine soy sauce and remaining ingredients, stirring well; pour over roast, and secure bag tightly. Place bag in a large shallow container; marinate in refrigerator 6 to 8 hours, turning bag occasionally.

Remove roast from marinade, reserving marinade. Thread roast on spit; secure with prongs at each end of spit. Balance roast properly to avoid strain on motor. Place spit on rotisserie 3 to 4 inches from low coals. Grill 2½ to 3 hours or until meat thermometer inserted into thickest part of roast registers 160° (medium). Baste with marinade during last hour of grilling time. Remove roast from spit; let stand 15 minutes before slicing. Yield: 16 servings.

OVEN-BARBECUED CRANBERRY PORK ROAST

4 cups fresh cranberries
1 cup sugar
½ cup commercial barbecue sauce (or
   see Sauce chapter)
½ cup orange juice
1 (4- to 6-pound) pork loin roast

Wash and sort cranberries; drain well. Combine cranberries, sugar, barbecue sauce, and orange juice in a large saucepan, stirring well; bring to a boil, stirring constantly. Boil, without stirring, 5 minutes. Remove cranberry mixture from heat, and set aside.

Place roast, fat side up, on a rack in a shallow roasting pan. Insert meat thermometer into thickest part of roast, making sure it does not touch bone or fat. Bake at 325° for 3 to 3½ hours or until thermometer registers 160° (medium). Baste frequently with cranberry mixture during last 30 minutes of baking time.

Let roast stand 15 minutes before slicing. Bring remaining cranberry mixture to a boil. Remove from heat. Serve roast with remaining cranberry mixture. Yield: 6 to 10 servings.

MARINATED PORK TENDERLOINS

2 (¾-pound) pork tenderloins, trimmed
1 (15-ounce) can sliced pineapple, undrained
2 tablespoons minced fresh gingerroot
2 tablespoons soy sauce
2 cloves garlic, minced
½ teaspoon dry mustard
Garnish: fresh parsley sprigs

Place tenderloins in a large shallow container. Drain pineapple, reserving juice; set pineapple slices aside. Combine juice, gingerroot, soy sauce, garlic, and mustard, stirring well; pour over tenderloins. Cover and marinate in refrigerator 6 to 8 hours, turning tenderloins occasionally.

Remove tenderloins from marinade. Insert meat thermometer into one tenderloin, making sure it does not touch fat. Grill tenderloins over medium coals 30 to 40 minutes or until thermometer registers 160° (medium). Turn tenderloins occasionally. Let stand 15 minutes before slicing.

Grill pineapple over medium coals 1 minute on each side. Slice tenderloins; serve with pineapple. Garnish, if desired. Yield: 6 servings.

MARINATED PORK STEAKS

4 (¾-inch-thick) pork blade steaks
1 (8¼-ounce) can sliced pineapple, undrained
1 medium onion, chopped
½ cup soy sauce
¼ cup vegetable oil
3 tablespoons light corn syrup
1 teaspoon ground ginger

Trim excess fat from steaks, and place steaks in a large shallow container. Drain pineapple, reserving syrup; set pineapple slices aside.

Combine pineapple syrup, chopped onion, soy sauce, oil, corn syrup, and ginger in a small saucepan, stirring well. Cook, uncovered, over medium heat 10 minutes, stirring frequently; pour mixture over steaks. Cover and marinate in refrigerator 6 to 8 hours, turning steaks occasionally.

Remove steaks from marinade, reserving marinade. Grill steaks over low to medium coals 35 minutes or until desired degree of doneness. Turn and baste occasionally with marinade.

Grill reserved pineapple slices over medium coals 1 minute on each side. Garnish pork steaks with pineapple slices. Yield: 4 servings.

BARBECUED HAM

1 cup pineapple juice
¼ cup plus 1 tablespoon firmly packed brown sugar
1 tablespoon dry mustard
2 tablespoons lemon juice
1 teaspoon onion salt
2 teaspoons soy sauce
2 (½-inch-thick) slices smoked ham (about ¾ pound)
1 (8¼-ounce) can sliced pineapple, drained

Combine first 6 ingredients in a medium saucepan, stirring well; bring to a boil. Reduce heat, and simmer, uncovered, 5 minutes; stir frequently. Remove sauce from heat, and set aside.

Trim excess fat from ham. Grill ham over medium coals 20 to 25 minutes or until desired degree of doneness. Turn and baste ham every 5 minutes with reserved sauce.

Grill pineapple slices over medium coals 1 minute on each side. Bring remaining sauce to a boil in a saucepan. Remove from heat.

Garnish ham with pineapple slices, and serve with remaining sauce. Yield: 3 to 4 servings.

COUNTRY-PRIDE PORK CHOPS

4 (1-inch-thick) center-cut pork chops
½ cup soy sauce
¼ cup firmly packed brown sugar
¼ cup sherry
1 teaspoon ground cinnamon
½ teaspoon garlic salt
Dash of ground ginger

Trim excess fat from pork chops, and place chops in a large shallow container. Combine soy sauce and remaining ingredients, stirring well; pour over chops. Cover and marinate in refrigerator 6 to 8 hours, turning frequently.

Remove chops from marinade, reserving marinade. Grill chops over medium coals 15 minutes on each side or until desired degree of doneness. Baste frequently with marinade. Yield: 4 servings.

MARINATED BARBECUED PORK CHOPS

6 to 8 (1-inch-thick) pork loin or rib
   chops
½ cup vegetable oil
¼ cup olive oil
¼ cup lemon juice
1 tablespoon salt
1 teaspoon paprika
½ teaspoon pepper
6 bay leaves, halved
3 cloves garlic, crushed

Trim excess fat from pork chops, and place chops in a large shallow container. Combine oil and remaining ingredients, stirring well; pour mixture over chops. Cover and marinate in refrigerator 6 to 8 hours, turning chops once.

Remove pork chops from marinade, reserving marinade. Grill over medium coals 40 to 45 minutes or until desired degree of doneness. Turn and baste occasionally with reserved marinade. Yield: 6 to 8 servings.

BARBECUED PORK CHOPS

1½ cups water
¾ cup catsup
¾ cup white vinegar
1 medium onion, chopped
1 clove garlic, minced
3 tablespoons brown sugar
1 tablespoon Worcestershire sauce
2 teaspoons salt
½ teaspoon pepper
¼ teaspoon hot sauce
8 (1¼-inch-thick) pork loin chops

Combine first 10 ingredients in a medium saucepan, stirring well; bring to a boil. Reduce heat, and simmer, uncovered, 30 minutes, stirring occasionally. Remove sauce from heat; set aside.

Trim excess fat from chops. Grill over medium coals 15 minutes on each side or until desired degree of doneness. Baste frequently with sauce. Bring remaining sauce to a boil in a saucepan. Remove from heat. Serve pork chops with remaining sauce. Yield: 8 servings.

GRILLED PORK CHOPS

¼ cup lemon juice
¼ cup butter or margarine
2 tablespoons Worcestershire sauce
¼ teaspoon salt
¼ teaspoon pepper
4 (1-inch-thick) pork chops

Combine all ingredients except chops in a small saucepan, stirring well; bring to a boil. Reduce heat, and simmer, uncovered, 15 minutes; stir occasionally. Remove sauce from heat; set aside.

Trim excess fat from chops. Grill chops over hot coals 20 minutes on each side or until desired degree of doneness. Baste frequently with sauce. Yield: 4 servings.

HICKORY-SMOKED STUFFED PORK CHOPS

Hickory chips
½ cup chopped onion
½ cup chopped celery
¼ cup butter or margarine, melted
1 cup herb-seasoned dressing mix
⅓ cup water
¼ teaspoon salt
¼ teaspoon pepper
4 (1½-inch-thick) pork loin chops
Liquid smoke

Soak hickory chips in water to cover for at least 30 minutes. Drain.

Sauté onion and celery in butter in a medium saucepan until tender. Add dressing mix, water, salt, and pepper, stirring well. Remove dressing mixture from heat, and set aside.

Trim excess fat from pork chops; make pockets in chops, cutting from rib side just to beginning of fat edge of each chop. Stuff pockets of chops with dressing mixture, and secure with wooden picks. Set aside.

Prepare charcoal fire in grill; let burn 30 to 45 minutes. Rake coals to one end of grill; place wood chips on hot coals. Place chops at opposite end. Grill, covered, over indirect heat 1 hour or until desired degree of doneness. Turn and sprinkle with liquid smoke every 15 minutes. Yield: 4 servings.

HAWAIIAN GRILLED PORK CHOPS

1 (20-ounce) can sliced pineapple, undrained
6 (1-inch-thick) pork chops
½ cup soy sauce
⅓ cup vegetable oil
¼ cup minced onion
1 clove garlic, minced
1 tablespoon brown sugar

Drain pineapple, reserving ¼ cup syrup. Set pineapple slices aside.

Trim excess fat from pork chops, and place chops in a large shallow container. Combine pineapple syrup, soy sauce, oil, onion, garlic, and sugar, stirring well; pour over chops. Cover and marinate in refrigerator 2 hours, turning once.

Remove chops from marinade, reserving marinade. Grill chops over medium coals 40 to 45 minutes or until desired degree of doneness. Turn and baste frequently with marinade.

Place a pineapple slice on each chop during last few minutes of grilling time. Yield: 6 servings.

OVEN-BARBECUED PORK CHOPS

6 (¾- to 1-inch-thick) pork chops
2 cups soy sauce
1 cup water
½ cup firmly packed brown sugar
1 tablespoon molasses
1 teaspoon salt
1 (14-ounce) bottle catsup
1 (12-ounce) bottle chili sauce
½ cup firmly packed brown sugar
⅓ cup water
1 tablespoon dry mustard

Trim excess fat from pork chops, and place chops in a large shallow container. Combine soy sauce, 1 cup water, ½ cup brown sugar, molasses, and salt, stirring well; pour mixture over chops. Cover and marinate in refrigerator 6 to 8 hours, turning chops occasionally.

Remove chops from marinade, and transfer to a 13- x 9- x 2-inch baking pan. Cover and bake at 350° for 1½ hours.

Combine catsup, chili sauce, ½ cup brown sugar, ⅓ cup water, and dry mustard in a medium saucepan; bring to a boil, stirring constantly.

Remove sauce from heat, and pour over pork chops; bake, uncovered, an additional 20 to 25 minutes or until tender. Serve pork chops with sauce. Yield: 6 servings.

APPLE-BARBECUED RIBS

6 pounds spareribs
½ cup chopped onion
1 clove garlic, minced
¼ cup vegetable oil
1 (16-ounce) can applesauce
½ cup catsup
⅓ cup chopped fresh parsley
2 tablespoons honey
2 tablespoons lemon juice
1 tablespoon Worcestershire sauce
1 teaspoon salt
1 teaspoon prepared mustard
½ teaspoon ground ginger
¼ teaspoon pepper

Cut ribs into serving-size pieces, and place in a large Dutch oven. Add water to cover; bring to a boil. Cover, reduce heat, and simmer 30 minutes. Drain ribs, and set aside.

Sauté onion and garlic in oil in a saucepan until tender. Stir in remaining ingredients; bring to a boil. Reduce heat, and simmer, uncovered, 15 minutes, stirring occasionally. Remove sauce from heat, and set aside.

Grill ribs over low coals 40 minutes, turning often. Baste ribs with sauce. Grill an additional 20 minutes. Turn and baste often with sauce. Bring remaining sauce to a boil in a saucepan. Remove from heat. Serve ribs with remaining sauce. Yield: 6 servings.

COUNTRY-STYLE RIBS

4 pounds country-style spareribs
1 onion, sliced
3 tablespoons butter or margarine
¼ cup finely chopped onion
1 clove garlic, minced
1 cup catsup
½ cup cider vinegar
Juice of ½ lemon
1 tablespoon sugar
2 tablespoons Worcestershire sauce
2 teaspoons prepared mustard
½ teaspoon salt
¼ teaspoon pepper

Cut ribs into 6 serving-size pieces, and place in a large Dutch oven. Add sliced onion and enough water to cover ribs; bring to a boil. Cover, reduce heat, and simmer 45 minutes. Drain ribs, and set aside.

Melt butter in a medium saucepan over low heat. Add chopped onion and garlic; sauté until tender.

Stir in catsup and remaining ingredients; bring mixture to a boil. Remove sauce from heat, and set aside.

Grill ribs over medium coals 20 to 30 minutes or until desired degree of doneness. Turn and baste frequently with sauce. Yield: 6 servings.

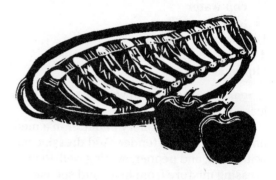

SPIT-ROASTED SPARERIBS

1 cup commercial barbecue sauce (or see Sauce chapter)
½ cup water
¼ cup molasses
¼ cup white vinegar
3 tablespoons Worcestershire sauce
2 teaspoons salt
½ teaspoon dry mustard
¼ teaspoon pepper
2 cloves garlic, minced
4 pounds spareribs

Combine all ingredients except spareribs, stirring well. Set sauce aside.

Cut ribs into serving-size pieces, and thread on spit; secure with prongs at each end of spit. Balance ribs properly to avoid strain on motor. Place spit on rotisserie 3 to 4 inches from low coals.

Grill ribs 1 hour or until desired degree of doneness. Baste with sauce during last 20 minutes of grilling time. Yield: 4 servings.

HICKORY-SMOKED BABY BACK PORK RIBS

3 slabs baby loin back ribs (about 5
  pounds)
¼ cup Dry Spice Rub (see page 44)
Hickory chunks
1 cup Vinegar Basting Sauce (see
  page 44)
1 cup Memphis-Style Barbecue Sauce (see
  page 44)

Place ribs in a large, shallow dish. Rub dry spices over ribs. Cover and refrigerate at least 3 hours.

Soak hickory chunks in water to cover for at least 1 hour.

Prepare charcoal fire in smoker; let burn 30 to 45 minutes or until coals are white. Place several soaked hickory chunks on coals. Place ribs on food rack, bone side down. (Do not add water pan.) Cover with smoker lid; cook 3 hours or until meat pulls away from the bone, turning and basting ribs with Vinegar Basting Sauce every 30 minutes. Replace hickory chunks every hour. Stir Memphis-Style Barbecue Sauce; brush ribs with barbecue sauce during last 30 minutes of cooking time. Yield: 4 to 6 servings.

TANGY BARBECUED COUNTRY-STYLE RIBS

¼ cup chopped onion
2 tablespoons vegetable oil
1 cup chili sauce
½ cup tomato juice
¼ cup firmly packed brown
  sugar
¼ cup lemon juice
2 tablespoons Worcestershire
  sauce
6 drops of hot sauce
3 pounds country-style spareribs
  or backbones
Salt and pepper to taste

Sauté onion in oil in a small saucepan until tender. Stir in chili sauce, tomato juice, sugar, lemon juice, Worcestershire sauce, and hot sauce; bring to a boil. Reduce heat, and simmer, uncovered, 15 to 20 minutes, stirring occasionally. Remove sauce from heat, and set aside.

Cut country-style ribs into 4 serving-size pieces, and sprinkle with salt and pepper to taste. Grill over low coals 45 minutes to 1 hour or until desired degree of doneness, turning frequently. Baste ribs with sauce during last 20 minutes of grilling time. Bring remaining sauce to a boil. Remove from heat, and serve with ribs. Yield: 4 servings.

TANGY MARINATED PORK KABOBS

2 pounds boneless pork, cut into 1-inch
  cubes
½ cup olive oil
¼ cup red wine vinegar
2 tablespoons soy sauce
1 teaspoon dry mustard
½ teaspoon celery seeds
½ teaspoon dried rosemary
½ teaspoon rubbed sage
Dash of pepper
2 cloves garlic, minced

Place pork in a large shallow container. Combine olive oil and remaining ingredients, stirring well; pour over pork. Cover and marinate in refrigerator 6 to 8 hours, stirring pork occasionally.

Remove pork from marinade, reserving marinade. Thread pork on skewers. Grill kabobs over medium coals 25 to 30 minutes or until desired degree of doneness, turning frequently. Baste kabobs with marinade during last 10 minutes of grilling time. Yield: 6 to 8 servings.

SOUTHERN TENDER KABOBS

2½ to 3 pounds boneless pork, cut into
   1½-inch cubes
½ cup soy sauce
¼ cup firmly packed brown sugar
2 tablespoons sherry
½ teaspoon garlic powder
½ teaspoon ground cinnamon
1 (12-ounce) jar red currant jelly
1 tablespoon prepared mustard
2 small tomatoes, quartered
2 small onions, peeled and quartered
1 medium-size green pepper, cut into
   1-inch pieces
½ pound fresh mushrooms

Place pork cubes in a large shallow container. Combine soy sauce, brown sugar, sherry, garlic powder, and cinnamon, stirring well; pour mixture over pork. Cover and marinate in refrigerator 3 to 4 hours, stirring pork occasionally.

Combine red currant jelly and mustard in a small saucepan; bring to a boil, stirring until jelly dissolves and mixture is blended. Remove jelly mixture from heat, and set aside.

Remove pork cubes from marinade. Thread pork on skewers. Alternate vegetables on separate skewers. Grill pork kabobs over medium coals 20 minutes, turning frequently. Place vegetable kabobs on grill. Grill vegetable and pork kabobs an additional 10 to 15 minutes or until desired degree of doneness. Turn and baste kabobs frequently with jelly mixture. Yield: 8 servings.

SWISS-HAM KABOBS

1 (20-ounce) can pineapple chunks,
   undrained
½ cup orange marmalade
1 tablespoon prepared mustard
¼ teaspoon ground cloves
1 pound fully cooked ham
½ pound Swiss cheese

Drain pineapple, reserving 2 tablespoons juice. Set chunks aside. Combine pineapple juice, orange marmalade, mustard, and cloves, stirring well. Set sauce aside.

Cut ham and Swiss cheese into 1½- x ½- x ½-inch pieces. Thread ham, cheese, ham, and pineapple chunks on skewers (cheese must be between and touching ham to prevent rapid melting).

Baste kabobs with reserved sauce, and grill over hot coals 3 to 4 minutes or until cheese is partially melted and ham is lightly browned. Turn and baste frequently with remaining sauce. Yield: 6 servings.

POULTRY

LEMON-BARBECUED TURKEY

1 (10- to 10½-pound) turkey, quartered
4 small cloves garlic, crushed
2 teaspoons salt
1¾ cups lemon juice
1 cup vegetable oil
½ cup chopped onion
2 teaspoons ground thyme
2 teaspoons pepper

Place turkey in a large shallow container. Mash garlic with salt in a medium bowl, using a fork. Add lemon juice and remaining ingredients, stirring well; pour over turkey. Cover and marinate in refrigerator 6 to 8 hours, turning turkey occasionally.

Remove turkey from marinade, reserving marinade. Prepare charcoal fire in grill. Place turkey, skin side down, on grill. Grill, covered, over medium coals 2 hours or until meat thermometer inserted into meaty part of thigh registers 185°, turning every 15 minutes. Baste turkey with marinade during last 30 minutes of grilling time. Let stand 15 minutes before slicing. Yield: about 10 servings.

SMOKED TURKEY ON THE WATER SMOKER

Mesquite chunks
1 (8- to 12-pound) turkey
2 tablespoons olive oil
1 tablespoon dried rosemary
2 teaspoons dried oregano
1 teaspoon dried basil
½ teaspoon dried thyme
2 bay leaves
4 cups apple cider or apple juice
¼ cup butter or margarine, melted
2 cloves garlic, chopped
2 teaspoons lemon juice

Soak mesquite chunks in water several hours. Remove giblets and neck from turkey; reserve for other uses, if desired. Rinse turkey with cold water; pat dry. Rub cavity with olive oil. Combine rosemary, oregano, basil, and thyme; stir well. Sprinkle cavity of turkey with herb mixture; add bay leaves. Tie ends of legs to tail with string or cord; lift wingtips up and over back so that they are tucked under bird.

Prepare charcoal fire in smoker, and let burn 30 to 45 minutes. Place mesquite chunks on coals. Place water pan in smoker. Combine apple cider, butter, garlic, and lemon juice; pour into water pan. Add enough hot water to fill water pan.

Place turkey on food rack. Cover with smoker lid; cook turkey 7 to 9 hours or until meat thermometer registers 185° when inserted in meaty part of thigh. (Make sure thermometer does not touch bone.) Refill water pan and add charcoal as needed. Remove turkey from smoker; let stand 15 minutes before slicing. Yield: 10 to 14 servings.

TEXAS-STYLE GAME HENS

½ cup apple jelly
½ cup catsup
1 tablespoon white vinegar
½ teaspoon chili powder
½ teaspoon salt
½ teaspoon garlic powder
½ teaspoon chili powder
4 (1- to 1¼-pound) Cornish hens, split

Combine first 4 ingredients in a small saucepan; stir well. Cook over medium heat until jelly melts, stirring constantly. Remove sauce from heat; keep warm.

Combine salt, garlic powder, and ½ teaspoon chili powder, stirring well; sprinkle over Cornish hens. Grill over medium coals 45 minutes; turn occasionally. Baste with sauce. Grill an additional 15 minutes. Turn and baste frequently with remaining sauce. Let stand 15 minutes before slicing. Yield: 4 servings.

CORNISH HENS ITALIANO

½ **cup butter or margarine**
½ **cup lime juice**
¼ **cup vegetable oil**
2 **(0.7-ounce) envelopes dry Italian salad dressing mix**
4 **(1- to 1¼-pound) Cornish hens**

Combine first 4 ingredients in a saucepan; stir well. Bring to a boil. Reduce heat, and simmer, uncovered, 5 minutes. Remove sauce from heat; keep warm.

Remove giblets from Cornish hens; reserve for other uses. Rinse hens thoroughly with cold water; pat dry. Fold neck skin over backs; secure with wooden picks. Lift wingtips up and over backs; tuck under hens. Close cavities, and secure with wooden picks; tie legs together with string.

Thread hens on spit; secure with prongs at each end of spit. Balance hens properly to avoid strain on motor. Place spit on rotisserie 4 to 6 inches from medium coals. Grill hens 1 hour and 15 minutes or until a meat thermometer registers 185° when inserted into meaty part of thigh. Baste frequently with sauce.

Remove hens from spit; let stand 15 minutes before slicing. Yield: 4 servings.

SMOKED CORNISH HENS

Mesquite chunks
4 **(1½-pound) Cornish hens**
2 **teaspoons Greek seasoning**
4 **slices bacon, cut in half**
2 **(12-ounce) cans beer**
10 **cups orange juice, divided**
Orange Liqueur Sauce
Dirty Rice
Garnishes: orange slices and fresh parsley sprigs

Soak mesquite chunks in water at least 2 hours before cooking.

Remove giblets from hens; reserve for other uses. Rinse hens with cold water, and pat dry. Lift wingtips up and over back of hens, tucking wingtips under hens. Close cavities with wooden picks or skewers, and tie legs together with string. Sprinkle hens with Greek seasoning. Crisscross 2 bacon slices over breast of each hen.

Prepare charcoal fire in smoker, and let burn 30 to 45 minutes. Place mesquite chunks on coals. Place water pan in smoker. Combine beer and 8 cups orange juice; pour into water pan.

Place hens on food rack. Cover with smoker lid; cook hens 5 to 6 hours or until meat thermometer registers 185° when inserted into meaty part of thigh. (Make sure thermometer does not touch bone.) Refill the water pan with remaining orange juice, and add charcoal as needed.

Remove hens from food rack, and place on a serving platter. Spoon Orange Liqueur Sauce over hens. Spoon Dirty Rice around hens. Garnish, if desired. Yield: 4 servings.

Orange Liqueur Sauce:
1 **medium onion, chopped**
1 **clove garlic, minced**
½ **cup butter or margarine, melted**
⅔ **cup Grand Marnier or other orange-flavored liqueur**
½ **cup honey**
2 **tablespoons lemon juice**
1 **tablespoon Worcestershire sauce**
1 **teaspoon ground ginger**
½ **teaspoon ground allspice**
2 **tablespoons cornstarch**
½ **cup orange juice**

Sauté onion and garlic in butter in a medium saucepan over medium-high heat until tender. Add Grand Marnier and next 5 ingredients; stir well. Bring to a boil.

Dissolve cornstarch in orange juice. Add to onion mixture, and bring to a boil. Cook 1 minute or until thickened, stirring constantly. Remove from heat. Yield: 2½ cups.

Dirty Rice:
5 **slices bacon**
1 **medium onion, chopped**
1 **(6-ounce) package long-grain and wild rice mix**
2⅓ **cups water**
1 **tablespoon butter or margarine**
½ **cup chopped pecans**

Cook bacon in a large skillet until crisp; remove bacon, reserving drippings in skillet. Crumble bacon, and set aside.

Sauté onion in drippings in skillet until tender. Set aside.

Combine rice mix, water, and butter in a saucepan. Bring to a boil; cover, reduce heat, and simmer 10 minutes. Stir in reserved bacon, onion, and pecans. Cover, and simmer an additional 15 minutes or until rice is tender and liquid is absorbed. Yield: 4 cups.

CAJUN-RUBBED CORNISH HENS

2 tablespoons garlic powder
1½ tablespoons onion powder
2½ tablespoons hot paprika
2 tablespoons coarsely ground pepper
1 tablespoon ground red pepper
1 tablespoon dried thyme
1 tablespoon dried oregano
4 (1½-pound) Cornish hens
2 tablespoons butter or margarine, melted
1 small onion, quartered
4 fresh parsley sprigs
4 cloves garlic

Combine first 7 ingredients in a small bowl; stir well.

Remove giblets from hens; reserve for other uses. Rinse hens with cold water, and pat dry. Brush outside of hens with melted butter, and rub with spice mixture.

Stuff hens with onion quarters, parsley sprigs, and garlic cloves; close cavities. Secure with wooden picks, and tie legs together with string.

Grill hens over medium coals 1½ to 2 hours, turning occasionally, or until meat thermometer registers 185° when inserted in meaty part of thigh. Serve immediately. Yield: 4 servings.

HONEY-BARBECUED CHICKEN

1 (2½- to 3-pound) broiler-fryer, split
¾ cup butter or margarine, melted
⅓ cup white vinegar
¼ cup honey
2 cloves garlic, minced
2 teaspoons salt
½ teaspoon dry mustard
Dash of pepper

Place chicken in a large shallow container. Combine melted butter and remaining ingredients, stirring well.

Grill chicken, skin side up, over hot coals 30 to 35 minutes or until done. Turn and baste frequently with sauce mixture. Yield: 4 servings.

SAUCY CHICKEN

2 (2½- to 3-pound) broiler-fryers, split
1 cup vegetable oil
½ cup white vinegar
¼ cup chili sauce
1 tablespoon prepared horseradish
1 teaspoon salt
½ teaspoon dry mustard
1 small clove garlic, crushed

Place chicken in 2 large shallow containers. Combine oil and remaining ingredients, stirring well; pour over chicken. Cover and marinate in refrigerator 2 hours, turning chicken occasionally.

Remove chicken from marinade, reserving marinade. Grill chicken pieces over low coals 45 minutes or until done. Turn and baste chicken frequently with marinade. Yield: 8 servings.

LEMON-BARBECUED CHICKEN

2 (2½- to 3-pound) broiler-fryers, split
1 cup vegetable oil
½ cup lemon juice
1 tablespoon salt
2 teaspoons onion powder
2 teaspoons dried basil
1 teaspoon paprika
½ teaspoon dried thyme
1 clove garlic, crushed
1 lemon, sliced

Place chicken in 2 large shallow containers. Combine oil and remaining ingredients, stirring well; pour over chicken. Cover and marinate in refrigerator 6 to 8 hours, turning chicken occasionally.

Remove chicken from marinade, reserving marinade. Grill chicken, skin side up, over low coals 20 to 25 minutes. Baste frequently with marinade. Turn chicken, and grill an additional 20 minutes or until done. Yield: 8 servings.

BARBECUED CHICKEN

Mesquite or oak chunks
2 (2½- to 3-pound) broiler-fryers
1 tablespoon lemon-pepper seasoning
1 tablespoon seasoned pepper
¼ teaspoon garlic powder
3 cups commercial barbecue sauce (or see Sauce chapter)

Soak mesquite chunks in water several hours before grilling. Remove giblets and necks from chicken; reserve for other uses. Rinse chicken with cold water; pat dry with paper towels. Close cavity with skewers; tie ends of legs together with string or cord. Lift wingtips up and over backs of chicken, tucking wingtips under chicken. Insert meat thermometer into meaty part of thigh of one chicken, making sure it does not touch bone.

Combine lemon-pepper seasoning, seasoned pepper, and garlic powder in a small bowl; sprinkle over chickens.

Prepare charcoal fire in one end of grill; let burn 30 to 45 minutes. Place wood chunks on coals. Place chickens on grill opposite hot coals. Grill, covered, over indirect heat 45 minutes. Baste with sauce. Cover and grill an additional 1 hour and 45 minutes, basting every 30 minutes with remaining sauce, or until thermometer registers 185°. Add more charcoal as needed. Let stand 15 minutes before slicing. Yield: 8 servings.

EASY BARBECUED CHICKEN

Hickory chunks
2 tablespoons salt
2 tablespoons paprika
1½ teaspoons pepper
4 (3- to 3½-pound) broiler-fryers, split
3 tablespoons vegetable oil
1 tablespoon white vinegar
1 teaspoon hot sauce

Soak hickory chunks in water to cover for at least 1 hour. Drain.

Combine salt, paprika, and pepper, stirring well; sprinkle over chicken. Combine oil, vinegar, and hot sauce, stirring well. Set chicken and oil mixture aside.

Prepare charcoal fire in grill; let burn 30 to 45 minutes. Rake coals to one end of grill; place wood chips on hot coals. Place chicken at opposite end of grill. Grill, covered, over indirect heat 3 to 3½ hours or until done, turning chicken occasionally. Baste chicken with oil mixture during last hour of grilling time. Yield: 16 servings.

OUTDOOR BARBECUED CHICKEN

2 cloves garlic
1 teaspoon salt
½ cup vegetable oil
½ cup lemon juice or white vinegar
½ cup water
¼ cup finely grated onion
1 teaspoon pepper
2 teaspoons Worcestershire sauce
2 (2½- to 3-pound) broiler-fryers, quartered

Mash garlic with salt in a small bowl, using a fork; stir in oil, lemon juice, water, onion, pepper, and Worcestershire sauce. Cover and chill sauce 24 hours.

Grill chicken over low coals 45 minutes or until done. Turn and baste frequently with sauce. Yield: 8 servings.

OLD SOUTH ZESTY BARBECUED CHICKEN

1 cup vegetable oil
½ cup white vinegar
½ teaspoon salt
¼ teaspoon pepper
⅛ teaspoon paprika
1 (3- to 3½-pound) broiler-fryer, quartered

Combine first 5 ingredients in a small bowl, stirring well. Set sauce aside.

Grill chicken, skin side down, over medium coals 50 to 60 minutes or until done, turning every 10 minutes. Baste chicken with sauce during last 20 minutes of grilling time. Yield: 4 servings.

PICNIC BARBECUED CHICKEN

2 cloves garlic, crushed
2 teaspoons butter or margarine, melted
1 cup catsup
¾ cup chili sauce
¼ cup firmly packed brown sugar
1 tablespoon celery seeds
1 tablespoon prepared mustard
2 tablespoons Worcestershire sauce
2 dashes of hot sauce
½ teaspoon salt
2 (2½- to 3-pound) broiler-fryers, quartered

Sauté garlic in melted butter in a saucepan until golden. Stir in catsup and next 7 ingredients; bring to a boil. Remove barbecue sauce from heat, and set aside.

Grill chicken, skin side up, over medium coals 15 minutes. Baste with reserved barbecue sauce. Grill an additional 40 minutes or until done. Baste every 10 minutes with remaining sauce. Yield: 8 servings.

HONEY-GLAZED CHICKEN

½ cup soy sauce
½ cup honey
1 teaspoon garlic powder
2 teaspoons dry mustard
1 teaspoon grated lemon rind
2 tablespoons lemon juice
½ teaspoon ground ginger
¼ teaspoon seasoned pepper
1 (3- to 3½-pound) broiler-fryer, cut up

Combine all ingredients except chicken, stirring well. Set sauce aside.

Grill chicken, skin side down, over medium coals 50 to 60 minutes or until done, turning chicken pieces every 10 minutes. Baste with sauce during last 20 minutes of grilling time. Yield: 4 servings.

SAVORY BARBECUED CHICKEN

1½ cups catsup
1⅓ cups pickle relish, drained
¼ cup firmly packed brown sugar
¼ cup soy sauce
2 tablespoons prepared mustard
¼ teaspoon pepper
2 cloves garlic, minced
2 (3- to 3½-pound) broiler-fryers, cut up

Combine all ingredients except chicken, stirring well. Set sauce aside.

Grill chicken, skin side down, over medium coals 1 hour or until done, turning chicken pieces every 10 minutes. Baste chicken with sauce during last 25 minutes of grilling time. Yield: 8 servings.

LEMONADE CHICKEN

1 (6-ounce) can frozen lemonade
  concentrate, thawed and undiluted
½ cup soy sauce
1 teaspoon seasoned salt
½ teaspoon celery salt
⅛ teaspoon garlic powder
2 (2½- to 3-pound) broiler-fryers, cut up

Combine all ingredients except chicken, stirring well. Set sauce aside.

Grill chicken over medium-hot coals 15 to 20 minutes, turning frequently. Baste with sauce. Grill chicken an additional 30 to 35 minutes or until done. Turn and baste pieces frequently with remaining sauce. Yield: 8 servings.

DIXIE STUFFED CHICKEN BREASTS

8 chicken breast halves, skinned and
  boned
½ teaspoon seasoned salt
¼ teaspoon poultry seasoning
¼ teaspoon pepper
1 (4½-ounce) can deviled ham
1 cup soft breadcrumbs
2 teaspoons instant minced onion
½ cup butter or margarine
1 (0.7-ounce) envelope dry Parmesan
  salad dressing mix

Place each chicken breast half on a sheet of wax paper; flatten to ¼-inch thickness, using a meat mallet or rolling pin.

Combine salt, poultry seasoning, and pepper, stirring well; sprinkle over chicken. Combine deviled ham, breadcrumbs, and onion, stirring well.

Spread mixture evenly over chicken breast halves, and roll up, jellyroll fashion, starting with short sides. Secure with wooden picks. Combine butter and salad dressing mix in a small saucepan. Cook, uncovered, over low heat until butter melts, stirring frequently. Remove sauce from heat.

Baste chicken with sauce. Grill over medium coals 20 minutes, basting frequently. Turn chicken, and baste with remaining

sauce. Grill an additional 20 minutes or until done. Yield: 8 servings.

GRILLED CHICKEN BREASTS

2 teaspoons Dijon mustard
4 chicken breast halves, skinned
¼ teaspoon freshly ground pepper
⅓ cup butter or margarine
1 teaspoon dried tarragon
2 teaspoons lemon juice
½ teaspoon garlic salt

Spread mustard on both sides of chicken, and sprinkle with pepper. Cover and refrigerate 2 to 4 hours.

Melt butter in a small saucepan over low heat; stir in remaining ingredients. Cook, uncovered, over low heat 5 minutes, stirring occasionally. Remove sauce from heat.

Baste chicken with sauce. Grill over medium coals 50 to 55 minutes or until done. Turn and baste every 10 minutes with remaining sauce. Yield: 4 servings.

FLAVORFUL BARBECUED CHICKEN

Hickory chips
2 cups white vinegar
½ cup plus 2 tablespoons shortening
½ cup butter or margarine
3 tablespoons ground black pepper
2 tablespoons ground red pepper
1 tablespoon plus 1½ teaspoons salt
8 chicken breast halves

Soak hickory chips in water to cover at least 30 minutes. Drain.

Combine vinegar and next 5 ingredients in a medium saucepan; bring to a boil. Reduce heat, and simmer sauce, uncovered, until shortening and butter melt. Remove sauce from heat.

Prepare fire in grill; let burn 30 to 45 minutes. Place wood chips on hot coals. Baste chicken with sauce, and grill over medium coals 45 to 55 minutes or until done. Turn and baste every 10 minutes with remaining sauce. Yield: 8 servings.

CHICKEN NAPOLI

1 cup butter or margarine
⅓ cup lime juice
2 (0.7-ounce) envelopes dry Italian salad
   dressing mix
8 chicken breast halves

Melt butter in a small saucepan over low heat; stir in lime juice and salad dressing mix. Remove sauce from heat. Baste chicken with sauce, and grill, skin side down, over medium coals 40 minutes or until done. Turn and baste often with sauce. Yield: 8 servings.

GRILLED CHICKEN

8 chicken breast halves, skinned
2 cups soy sauce
1 cup vegetable oil
½ cup white vinegar
¼ cup firmly packed brown sugar
1 tablespoon dried oregano
1 tablespoon dried thyme
2 teaspoons dry mustard

Place chicken in a Dutch oven. Add water to cover; bring to a boil. Cover, reduce heat, and simmer 15 minutes. Drain chicken, and place in a large shallow container. Combine soy sauce and remaining ingredients, stirring well; pour marinade over chicken. Cover and marinate in refrigerator 4 hours, turning chicken frequently.

Remove chicken from marinade. Grill over medium coals 10 to 15 minutes or until done, turning once. Yield: 8 servings.

RUMAKI KABOBS

2 large carrots, cut into ½-inch pieces
12 chicken livers (about 1 pound)
½ cup soy sauce
¼ cup firmly packed brown sugar
¼ teaspoon ground ginger
8 whole water chestnuts
12 slices bacon, cut in half
2 medium onions, quartered
1 large green pepper, cut into 1-inch
   pieces
Hot cooked rice

Cook carrots 1 minute in boiling water to cover. Drain and set aside.

Cut chicken livers in half. Dip each half into soy sauce. Combine remaining soy sauce, sugar, and ginger, stirring until sugar dissolves. Set chicken livers and soy sauce mixture aside.

Cut water chestnuts into thirds. Place a piece of water chestnut and a piece of chicken liver on each piece of bacon; roll up. Alternate chicken liver bundles and vegetables on skewers.

Grill kabobs 15 to 20 minutes over medium coals or until chicken livers are done. Turn and baste frequently with soy sauce mixture. Serve over hot cooked rice. Yield: 4 servings.

SESAME CHICKEN KABOBS

2 whole chicken breasts, skinned, boned,
   and cut into 1-inch cubes
¼ cup soy sauce
¼ cup commercial Russian salad
   dressing
1 tablespoon sesame seeds
2 tablespoons lemon juice
¼ teaspoon garlic powder
¼ teaspoon ground ginger
1 green pepper, cut into 1-inch pieces
2 medium onions, cut into eighths
3 small zucchini, cut into ¾-inch pieces
1 pint cherry tomatoes

Place chicken cubes in a large shallow container. Combine soy sauce, dressing, sesame seeds, lemon juice, garlic powder, and ginger in a jar; cover tightly, and shake vigorously. Pour mixture over chicken. Cover and marinate in refrigerator 2 hours, stirring chicken occasionally.

Remove chicken from marinade, reserving marinade. Alternate chicken and vegetables on skewers. Grill kabobs over medium-hot coals 15 to 20 minutes or until chicken is done. Turn and baste frequently with marinade. Yield: 6 servings.

HAWAIIAN KABOBS

1½ pounds boneless chicken breasts, cut
   into 1-inch cubes
1 (15¼-ounce) can pineapple chunks,
   undrained
½ cup soy sauce
¼ cup vegetable oil
1 tablespoon brown sugar
1 teaspoon garlic powder
2 teaspoons ground ginger
1 teaspoon dry mustard
¼ teaspoon freshly ground pepper
1 large green pepper, cut into 1-inch
   pieces
12 medium-size fresh mushrooms
18 cherry tomatoes
Hot cooked rice

Place chicken cubes in a large shallow container. Drain pineapple, reserving ½ cup juice. Set pineapple chunks aside.

Combine pineapple juice, soy sauce, oil, sugar, garlic powder, ginger, dry mustard, and pepper in a small saucepan, stirring well; bring to a boil. Reduce heat, and simmer, uncovered, 5 minutes.

Pour mixture over chicken. Cover and marinate in refrigerator 1 hour, stirring chicken occasionally.

Remove chicken from marinade, reserving marinade. Alternate chicken, pineapple, green pepper, mushrooms, and tomatoes on skewers. Grill kabobs over hot coals 20 minutes or until chicken is done. Turn and baste frequently with marinade. Serve over hot cooked rice. Yield: 6 servings.

SAUCES & MARINADES

DRESSED-UP BARBECUE SAUCE

1 (18-ounce) bottle commercial barbecue
    sauce with onion bits
⅔ cup firmly packed brown sugar
½ cup Burgundy or other dry
    red wine
1 teaspoon Worcestershire sauce
Dash of hot sauce

Combine all ingredients, stirring well. Use sauce to baste chicken or lamb when grilling. Yield: 2½ cups.

1948 ORIGINAL BARBECUE SAUCE

1 medium onion, chopped
2 cloves garlic, minced
2 tablespoons butter or margarine,
    melted
1 (14½-ounce) can whole tomatoes
1 (8-ounce) can tomato sauce
½ cup chopped celery
⅓ cup white vinegar
¼ cup chopped green pepper
2 fresh celery leaves, chopped
1 bay leaf
3 tablespoons molasses
1½ teaspoons salt
2 teaspoons dry mustard
2 teaspoons hot sauce
½ teaspoon ground cloves
½ teaspoon ground allspice
2 lemon slices

Sauté onion and garlic in butter in a saucepan until tender. Stir in tomatoes and remaining ingredients; bring to a boil. Reduce heat, and simmer, uncovered, 30 minutes; stir occasionally. Remove and discard bay leaf and lemon slices.

Process mixture through a food mill or in a food processor, if desired.

Use sauce for basting, or serve with chicken. Yield: 3 cups.

WESTERN KENTUCKY-STYLE BARBECUE SAUCE

1¾ cups water
1 cup plus 2 tablespoons catsup
⅓ cup Worcestershire sauce
1½ teaspoons ground red pepper
1 teaspoon paprika
1 teaspoon dry mustard
¾ teaspoon garlic salt
¾ teaspoon onion powder
¾ teaspoon pepper

Combine all ingredients in a saucepan. Cook over medium heat 20 minutes. Use to baste chicken or ribs. Yield: about 3 cups.

TEXAS BARBECUE SAUCE

2 cups butter or margarine, softened
2 tablespoons dry mustard
1 (5-ounce) bottle Worcestershire sauce
¼ cup garlic-flavored wine vinegar
3 tablespoons lemon juice
2 teaspoons hot sauce
Salt to taste
Red pepper to taste

Combine butter and mustard in a medium bowl, stirring well. Stir in remaining ingredients. Cover and refrigerate sauce 24 hours. Heat thoroughly, and use to baste beef, pork, or chicken when grilling. Yield: 2½ cups.

HAWAIIAN BARBECUE SAUCE

¾ cup pineapple juice
½ cup vegetable oil
⅓ cup soy sauce
¼ cup lemon juice
¼ cup molasses
1 teaspoon ground ginger

Combine all ingredients, stirring well. Use sauce to baste chicken, pork, or lamb when grilling. Yield: 2 cups.

DRY SPICE RUB

3½ tablespoons paprika
2 teaspoons seasoned salt
2 teaspoons garlic powder
2 teaspoons black pepper
1 teaspoon ground red pepper
1 teaspoon dried oregano
1 teaspoon chili powder
½ teaspoon dry mustard

Combine paprika, seasoned salt, garlic powder, pepper, dried oregano, chili powder, and dry mustard in a small bowl; stir well. Yield: ¼ cup plus 2 tablespoons.

VINEGAR BASTING SAUCE

2 cups red wine vinegar
2 cups water
⅓ cup firmly packed brown sugar
¼ cup Worcestershire sauce
2 tablespoons Dry Spice Rub (see recipe above)
½ teaspoon hot sauce

Combine all ingredients in a medium-size bowl, stirring well. Cover and let mixture stand at room temperature 8 hours. Yield: 4½ cups.

MEMPHIS-STYLE BARBECUE SAUCE

1 (8-ounce) can tomato sauce
1 cup catsup
1 cup red wine vinegar
½ cup honey mustard
½ cup hickory-smoked Worcestershire sauce
3 tablespoons butter or margarine
2 tablespoons brown sugar
1 tablespoon paprika
1 tablespoon seasoned salt
1½ tablespoons hot sauce
1 tablespoon lemon juice
1½ teaspoons garlic powder
¼ teaspoon chili powder
⅛ teaspoon ground red pepper
⅛ teaspoon black pepper

Combine all ingredients in a large saucepan. Bring to a boil; reduce heat, cover and simmer 30 minutes, stirring occasionally. Yield: 4 cups.

LOW-COUNTRY BARBECUE SAUCE

2 cups chopped tomatoes
1 medium onion, finely chopped
¼ cup butter or margarine, melted
¼ cup white vinegar
1 tablespoon sugar
1 tablespoon paprika
1 tablespoon pepper
2 teaspoons salt
1½ teaspoons Worcestershire sauce
¼ teaspoon hot sauce
1 clove garlic
½ red pepper pod

Process tomatoes through a food mill or pulse several times in a food processor. Sauté onion in butter in a medium saucepan until tender. Stir in tomatoes, vinegar, and remaining ingredients; bring to a boil. Reduce heat, and simmer sauce, uncovered, 15 minutes, stirring occasionally. Remove and discard garlic and red pepper pod. Serve sauce over sliced pork. Yield: 2 cups.

FRESH TOMATO BARBECUE SAUCE

1 cup coarsely chopped onion
2 cloves garlic, minced
2 tablespoons butter or margarine, melted
5 small tomatoes, peeled and chopped
2 tablespoons Worcestershire sauce
2 tablespoons red wine vinegar
2 teaspoons salt
1 teaspoon chili powder
1 teaspoon dry mustard
½ cup dark corn syrup

Sauté onion and garlic in butter in a medium saucepan until tender. Stir in tomatoes and next 5 ingredients; bring to a boil. Reduce heat, and simmer sauce, uncovered, 20 minutes, stirring occasionally. Stir in corn syrup, and simmer, uncovered, an additional 10 minutes.

Use sauce for basting, or serve with beef or ribs. Yield: 3 cups.

PAPRIKA BARBECUE SAUCE

1 cup catsup
½ cup white vinegar
½ cup butter or margarine
¼ cup firmly packed brown sugar
¼ cup paprika
Juice of 2 lemons
1 tablespoon pepper
1 tablespoon plus 1 teaspoon prepared horseradish
2 teaspoons prepared mustard
1 teaspoon Worcestershire sauce
¼ teaspoon hot sauce
1 clove garlic, minced

Combine all ingredients in a large saucepan, stirring well; bring to a boil. Reduce heat, and simmer sauce, uncovered, 10 to 15 minutes, stirring occasionally.

Use sauce for basting, or serve with chicken, beef, or ribs. Yield: 2 cups.

HERB BUTTER SAUCE

2 tablespoons minced green onions
1 clove garlic, minced
½ cup butter, melted
2 tablespoons chopped fresh parsley
½ teaspoon dried tarragon
¼ teaspoon salt
¼ teaspoon pepper

Sauté green onions and garlic in butter in a skillet over medium heat until onion is tender. Remove from heat; stir in parsley and remaining ingredients.

Use sauce for basting or for sautéing poultry, fish, or vegetables. Yield: ½ cup.

MAGNIFICENT MARINADE

1½ cups vegetable oil
¾ cup soy sauce
½ cup red wine vinegar
⅓ cup lemon juice
¼ cup Worcestershire sauce
2 cloves garlic, crushed
2 tablespoons dry mustard
1 tablespoon coarsely ground pepper
2½ teaspoons salt
2 teaspoons chopped fresh parsley

Combine all ingredients in a medium bowl, stirring well. Store in an airtight container in refrigerator. Yield: 3½ cups.

BOURBON BARBECUE SAUCE

1 cup catsup
⅓ cup bourbon
¼ cup white vinegar
¼ cup molasses
2 cloves garlic, crushed
1 tablespoon Worcestershire sauce
1 tablespoon lemon juice
2 teaspoons soy sauce
½ teaspoon dry mustard
¼ teaspoon pepper

Combine all ingredients, stirring well. Use sauce to baste pork or beef when grilling. Yield: 2 cups.

BARBECUE SAUCE FOR CHICKEN

2 cups butter or margarine
1 cup white vinegar
½ (6-ounce) jar prepared mustard
¼ cup Worcestershire sauce

Melt butter in a saucepan over low heat. Stir in remaining ingredients; remove from heat. Cover and refrigerate sauce until ready to use. Heat thoroughly, and use to baste chicken when grilling. Yield: about 4 cups.

CREOLE BARBECUE SAUCE

2 cups water
2 cups white vinegar
½ cup butter or margarine
¼ cup sugar
¼ cup Worcestershire sauce
¼ cup catsup
2 drops of hot sauce
1 large purple onion, chopped
6 stalks celery, chopped
1 lemon, thinly sliced
1 bay leaf
1 tablespoon salt
2 tablespoons ground red pepper
2 tablespoons celery seeds
1 teaspoon garlic salt
1 teaspoon dry mustard
1 teaspoon pepper

Combine all ingredients in a Dutch oven, stirring well; bring to a boil. Reduce heat, and simmer sauce, uncovered, 30 minutes, stirring occasionally. Remove and discard bay leaf. Use sauce for basting, or serve with beef, pork, or chicken. Yield: about 7 cups.

MUSTARD BARBECUE SAUCE

2 cups prepared mustard
1 cup mayonnaise
½ cup water
¼ cup plus 2 tablespoons catsup
¼ cup butter or margarine
2 tablespoons sugar
2 tablespoons Worcestershire sauce
1 teaspoon browning-and-seasoning sauce
½ teaspoon salt
½ teaspoon seasoned salt
¼ teaspoon pepper
¼ teaspoon liquid smoke

Combine all ingredients in a small Dutch oven, stirring well; bring to a boil. Reduce heat, and simmer, uncovered, 10 minutes; stir occasionally.

Use barbecue sauce for basting, or serve with chicken, lamb, pork, or ribs. Yield: about 4 cups.

SALADS

MARINATED TOMATO SLICES

4 tomatoes, sliced
1 onion, thinly sliced
1 cup vegetable oil
⅓ cup red wine vinegar
⅛ teaspoon garlic powder
Salt and pepper to taste
Lettuce leaves (optional)

Arrange tomato and onion slices in a large shallow container. Combine oil, vinegar, and garlic powder, stirring well; pour over tomato and onion. Sprinkle with salt and pepper. Cover and refrigerate at least 1 hour. Serve on lettuce-lined salad plates, if desired. Yield: 6 servings.

MEDITERRANEAN SPRING SALAD

½ pound small new potatoes
½ cup olive oil
2 tablespoons lemon juice
1 clove garlic, crushed
2 teaspoons dried oregano
¼ teaspoon salt
6 cups mixed torn salad greens
2 small tomatoes, cut into wedges
1 small purple onion, thinly sliced and
    separated into rings
1 small cucumber, thinly sliced
½ cup crumbled feta cheese

Scrub potatoes. Cook in boiling salted water to cover 20 minutes or until tender; drain well, and cool. Peel and thinly slice potatoes; place in a shallow container.

Combine oil, juice, garlic, oregano, and salt, stirring well; pour over potatoes. Cover and refrigerate 1 hour. Drain potatoes, reserving marinade.

Place salad greens in a large salad bowl. Arrange potatoes, tomato, onion, cucumber, and cheese over top. Serve with marinade. Yield: 8 servings.

SIMPLY GOOD SALAD

2 cups torn spinach
2 cups torn iceberg lettuce
1 cup (4 ounces) shredded sharp
    Cheddar cheese
1 hard-cooked egg, chopped
1 small green onion, chopped
1 (8-ounce) can pineapple tidbits,
    drained
Commercial buttermilk-style salad
    dressing, chilled

Combine spinach, lettuce, cheese, egg, green onion, and pineapple in a large salad bowl; toss gently. Serve with salad dressing. Yield: 6 servings.

SEVEN-LAYER SALAD

1 small head lettuce, coarsely chopped or
    shredded
1½ cups chopped celery
1½ cups chopped green pepper
1½ cups chopped purple onion
3 (8½-ounce) cans small English peas,
    drained
2¼ cups mayonnaise
2 teaspoons sugar
Grated Parmesan cheese
6 slices bacon, cooked and crumbled

Layer lettuce, celery, green pepper, purple onion, and peas in a large salad bowl. Combine mayonnaise and sugar; spread mayonnaise mixture evenly over top. Sprinkle with remaining ingredients. Cover tightly, and chill 8 hours. Yield: 6 servings.

BOSTON TOSSED SALAD

½ cup olive oil
¼ cup corn oil
¼ cup red wine vinegar
½ teaspoon lemon-pepper
   seasoning
¼ teaspoon chopped fresh parsley
1 head Boston lettuce, torn
1 (11-ounce) can mandarin oranges,
   drained
½ small purple onion, thinly sliced and
   separated into rings
12 large fresh mushrooms, sliced

Combine first 5 ingredients in a jar. Cover tightly, and shake vigorously. Refrigerate dressing several hours.

Combine lettuce, oranges, onion, and sliced mushrooms in a salad bowl, tossing gently. Serve with chilled dressing. Yield: 6 servings.

SPINACH SALAD

½ cup vegetable oil
¼ cup sugar
¼ cup chili sauce
1 small onion, minced
2 tablespoons red wine vinegar
½ teaspoon salt
½ teaspoon dry mustard
½ teaspoon Worcestershire sauce
¼ teaspoon ground red pepper
1 pound spinach, torn
⅔ cup torn Bibb lettuce
1 hard-cooked egg, grated
¾ cup cooked and crumbled bacon

Combine first 9 ingredients in a jar. Cover tightly, and shake vigorously. Refrigerate dressing several hours.

Combine spinach and lettuce in a salad bowl. Sprinkle egg and crumbled bacon over top of salad. Serve with chilled dressing. Yield: 4 servings.

CRISPY COLESLAW

1 medium cabbage, shredded
1 small onion, minced
½ cup sweet pickle cubes
1 cup mayonnaise
¼ cup sugar
¼ cup white vinegar
1 tablespoon salt
1 teaspoon dillseeds
1 teaspoon celery seeds or celery salt
¼ teaspoon pepper
Leaf lettuce
Garnishes: green pepper rings, pimiento
   strips

Combine first 3 ingredients in a large bowl. Set cabbage mixture aside.

Combine mayonnaise, sugar, vinegar, and seasonings; stir well. Pour over cabbage mixture; toss well. Cover and refrigerate coleslaw several hours.

Serve coleslaw in a lettuce-lined bowl, and garnish, if desired. Yield: 12 servings.

COUNTRY-STYLE COLESLAW

1 large cabbage, coarsely chopped
1½ cups shredded carrots
1 cup chopped green pepper
¼ cup chopped green onions
1 cup mayonnaise
3 tablespoons sugar
3 tablespoons white vinegar
1½ teaspoons salt
¾ teaspoon dry mustard
¼ teaspoon celery seeds
Garnish: green pepper rings

Combine first 4 ingredients in a large bowl. Set cabbage mixture aside.

Combine mayonnaise, sugar, vinegar, salt, dry mustard, and celery seeds, stirring well; pour over cabbage mixture, and toss well. Cover and chill thoroughly. Garnish, if desired. Yield: 12 servings.

GERMAN POTATO SALAD

4 medium potatoes
8 slices bacon
⅓ cup water
⅓ cup white vinegar
¼ cup sugar
2 tablespoons all-purpose flour
1 small green pepper, chopped
1 small onion, chopped
¼ cup chopped celery
1 tablespoon chopped pimiento

Scrub potatoes. Cook in boiling water to cover 20 minutes or until tender. Drain and cool slightly. Peel potatoes; cut into ½-inch cubes, and set aside.

Cook bacon in a large skillet until crisp; remove bacon, reserving ¼ cup drippings in skillet. Crumble bacon, and set aside.

Add water, vinegar, sugar, and flour to drippings in skillet, stirring well. Cook over medium heat until mixture is slightly thickened. Remove vinegar mixture from heat, and set aside.

Combine potatoes, green pepper, onion, celery, and pimiento in a large bowl. Top with vinegar mixture, and toss gently. Sprinkle with crumbled bacon. Yield: 6 servings.

SOUR CREAM POTATO SALAD

6 to 8 medium potatoes
2 tablespoons sweet pickle relish
2 tablespoons finely chopped onion
2 tablespoons chopped fresh parsley
1 (2-ounce) jar chopped pimiento, drained
2 tablespoons white vinegar
1 tablespoon prepared mustard
1 teaspoon salt
Pepper to taste
1 (8-ounce) carton sour cream
1½ cups chopped celery
2 hard-cooked eggs, chopped

Scrub potatoes. Cook in boiling water to cover 20 to 30 minutes or until tender. Drain and cool. Peel potatoes; cut into ½-inch cubes, and set aside.

Combine pickle relish, onion, parsley, pimiento, vinegar, mustard, salt, and pepper in a large salad bowl, stirring well; fold in sour cream.

Add cubed potatoes, celery, and eggs; toss gently. Cover and chill 1 hour. Yield: 8 to 10 servings.

VEGETABLES

FANCY MUSHROOMS WITH CRABMEAT STUFFING

Mesquite chips
1 pound fresh lump crabmeat, drained
1 cup finely chopped green onions
½ cup soft breadcrumbs
¼ cup butter or margarine, melted
2 large eggs, beaten
2 tablespoons chopped fresh parsley
1 teaspoon dry mustard
1 teaspoon Worcestershire sauce
½ teaspoon salt
½ teaspoon Old Bay seasoning
⅛ teaspoon ground mace
⅛ teaspoon ground nutmeg
⅛ teaspoon pepper
24 large fresh mushrooms (1½ pounds)
Herb Butter Sauce (see page 45)

Soak mesquite chips in water to cover for 30 minutes. Combine crabmeat and next 12 ingredients in a medium bowl; stir well. Cover and chill mixture 1 hour.

Clean mushrooms with damp paper towels. Remove stems, and reserve for other uses. Sauté mushroom caps in Herb Butter Sauce in a large skillet over medium heat for 8 to 10 minutes. Remove mushrooms from skillet, and place about ½ inch apart in a lightly greased 13- x 9- x 2-inch disposable aluminum pan. Spoon chilled crabmeat mixture evenly into mushroom caps.

Place soaked mesquite chips on hot coals or heating element of an electric grill. Grill mushrooms, covered, over medium coals 15 minutes or until heated. Yield: 12 servings.

SAUTÉED AND GRILLED MUSHROOMS

Mesquite or hickory chips
24 large fresh mushrooms (1 ½ pounds)
Herb Butter Sauce (see page 45)

Soak wood chips and 6 (12-inch) wooden skewers in water for at least 30 minutes.

Sauté mushrooms in Herb Butter Sauce in a large skillet over medium-high heat 8 minutes. Remove from heat; let mushrooms cool slightly. Thread mushrooms onto skewers. Reserve remaining Herb Butter Sauce.

Prepare charcoal fire, and let burn 30 to 45 minutes. Place mesquite chips on coals or on heating element of an electric grill. Brush mushrooms with reserved Herb Butter Sauce. Grill mushrooms, covered, over medium coals 5 minutes. Brush with remaining Herb Butter Sauce. Turn and grill, covered, an additional 5 minutes. Yield: 6 servings.

HERB-SEASONED GREEN BEANS

1½ pounds fresh green beans
¾ teaspoon salt
1½ cups water
¾ cup chopped onion
¼ cup plus 2 tablespoons chopped celery
1 large clove garlic, minced
3 tablespoons butter or margarine
¾ teaspoon dried rosemary
¾ teaspoon dried basil

Remove strings from beans; cut beans into 1-inch pieces. Wash beans. Place beans, salt, and water in a large saucepan; bring to a boil. Cover, reduce heat, and simmer 10 minutes. Stir in onion and remaining ingredients; cover and cook an additional 10 to 15 minutes or until tender. Yield: 6 servings.

CORN-ON-THE-COB WITH HERB BUTTER

½ cup butter or margarine, softened
2 tablespoons chopped fresh parsley
2 tablespoons chopped fresh chives
½ teaspoon dried salad herbs
8 ears fresh corn
About 1 gallon water

Combine first 4 ingredients, stirring well. Set butter mixture aside. Remove husks and silks from corn just before cooking. Bring water to a boil in a Dutch oven; add corn. Return to a boil, and boil 8 to 10 minutes. Drain well. Spread butter mixture over hot corn. Yield: 8 servings.

CORN PUDDING

2 cups fresh corn, cut from cob
¼ cup all-purpose flour
2 to 3 tablespoons sugar
1 teaspoon salt
2 cups milk
2 eggs, beaten
2 tablespoons butter or margarine, melted

Combine corn, flour, sugar, and salt in a large bowl, stirring well. Combine milk and remaining ingredients, stirring well; add to corn mixture.

Pour corn mixture into a lightly greased 1½-quart casserole. Bake at 350° for 1 hour, stirring twice during first 30 minutes. Yield: 6 servings.

HERBED POTATOES ON THE GRILL

¼ cup finely chopped celery
¾ cup butter or margarine, melted
1 teaspoon dried oregano
½ teaspoon salt
¼ teaspoon garlic powder
⅛ teaspoon pepper
6 medium-size baking potatoes, unpeeled
1 medium onion, thinly sliced
Paprika
Garnish: fresh oregano sprigs

Sauté celery in butter in a small saucepan until tender. Stir in dried oregano, salt, garlic powder, and pepper. Remove butter mixture from heat, and keep warm.

Wash potatoes; cut each into ½-inch slices, cutting to, but not through, bottom peel.

Place a slice of onion between each slice of potato. Place each potato on a square of heavy-duty aluminum foil; drizzle about 2 tablespoons butter mixture over each. Fold foil edges over, and wrap securely.

Grill foil-wrapped potatoes over medium coals 45 minutes to 1 hour or until potatoes are tender. Unwrap potatoes, and sprinkle lightly with paprika. Garnish, if desired. Yield: 6 servings.

PARSLEY NEW POTATOES

1½ pounds new potatoes
2½ cups water
Salt to taste
¼ cup plus 2 tablespoons butter or margarine, melted
3 tablespoons chopped fresh parsley

Wash potatoes; peel a strip around center of each potato, if desired.

Combine potatoes, water, and salt in a large saucepan; bring to a boil. Cover, reduce heat, and cook 15 minutes or until potatoes are tender. Drain well; transfer potatoes to a serving bowl.

Combine butter and parsley, stirring well. Spoon butter mixture over hot potatoes. Yield: 4 servings.

CHARCOAL-BAKED POTATOES

6 medium-size baking potatoes, unpeeled
Butter, margarine, or sour cream
Salt and pepper to taste

Wrap each potato securely in heavy-duty aluminum foil. Place foil-wrapped potatoes around gray coals on bottom of grill.

Cook 1 hour and 15 minutes or until potatoes are tender. Turn potatoes every 20 minutes, using hot pads or tongs.

Unwrap potatoes, and cut a slit in top of each. Press sides to loosen potato pulp. Add butter or sour cream; sprinkle with salt and pepper to taste. Serve hot. Yield: 6 servings.

ZIPPY ZUCCHINI SKILLET

2 tablespoons vegetable oil
4 medium zucchini, thinly sliced
1 medium onion, chopped
1 (16-ounce) can whole kernel corn, drained
1 (4-ounce) can chopped green chiles
2 teaspoons seeded and chopped jalapeño peppers
1/4 teaspoon salt
1/8 teaspoon garlic powder
1/2 cup (2 ounces) shredded Cheddar cheese

Heat oil in a large skillet; add zucchini and onion, and sauté 10 minutes or until tender. Stir in corn and next 4 ingredients; cook, stirring occasionally, until thoroughly heated. Remove from heat; stir in cheese. Yield: 6 servings.

CHEESY STUFFED SQUASH

6 medium-size yellow squash
1/2 pound bacon
1 small onion, chopped
3/4 cup soft breadcrumbs
1 cup (4 ounces) shredded sharp Cheddar cheese
Paprika

Wash squash thoroughly, and cook in boiling salted water to cover for 8 to 10 minutes or until tender but still firm. Drain squash and cool slightly. Remove and discard stems. Cut each squash in half lengthwise; remove and reserve pulp, leaving a firm shell.

Cook bacon in a large skillet until crisp; drain well, reserving 2 tablespoons bacon drippings in skillet. Crumble bacon, and set aside. Sauté onion in bacon drippings until tender; stir in crumbled bacon, breadcrumbs, and squash pulp.

Place squash shells in a 13- x 9- x 2-inch baking dish. Spoon squash mixture evenly into shells, and top with cheese. Broil 6 inches from heat about 5 minutes or just until cheese is melted. Sprinkle with paprika. Yield: 6 servings.

EASY SUCCOTASH

2 cups fresh lima beans (about 1 pound)
4 cups fresh corn, cut from cob (about 8 ears)
1/2 cup whipping cream
3 tablespoons butter or margarine
1/2 teaspoon salt
1/8 teaspoon pepper

Cook beans in boiling salted water to cover for 15 minutes or until almost tender; drain. Add corn and remaining ingredients; stir well. Cook, uncovered, over low heat 8 to 10 minutes or until corn is done; stir frequently. Yield: 6 servings.

SUMMER GARDEN MEDLEY

2 tablespoons chopped onion
1 tablespoon butter or margarine, melted
1 cup fresh corn, cut from cob
2 small tomatoes, peeled and cubed
2 small yellow squash, sliced
1/2 teaspoon salt
1/4 teaspoon sugar
1/4 teaspoon dried oregano
1/8 teaspoon pepper

Sauté onion in butter in a small Dutch oven until tender. Add corn and remaining ingredients, stirring well. Cover and cook over medium heat 15 minutes or until all vegetables are tender. Yield: 4 servings.

VEGETABLES IN A PACKET

3 medium tomatoes, quartered
3 medium-size yellow squash, sliced
1 small onion, sliced
1 teaspoon minced fresh basil
1/2 teaspoon salt
1/8 teaspoon pepper
2 teaspoons butter or margarine

Place tomato, squash, and onion on a large piece of heavy-duty aluminum foil; sprinkle with basil, salt, and pepper. Dot with butter. Fold foil edges over, and wrap securely. Grill packet over medium coals 20 to 25 minutes, turning after 10 minutes. Yield: 4 servings.

BREADS

MEXICAN CORNBREAD

1 tablespoon vegetable oil
1½ cups self-rising cornmeal
1 cup buttermilk
2 large eggs, beaten
3 tablespoons vegetable oil
1 (8¾-ounce) can cream-style corn
½ cup chopped green pepper
6 slices bacon, cooked and crumbled
¼ cup chopped canned jalapeño peppers
Dash of garlic powder
2 cups (8 ounces) shredded sharp
   Cheddar cheese, divided

Grease a 10½-inch cast-iron skillet with 1 tablespoon oil. Heat at 350° for 10 minutes or until very hot. Combine cornmeal and next 8 ingredients; stir well. Pour half of cornmeal mixture into skillet. Sprinkle with 1 cup cheese. Top with remaining cornmeal mixture. Bake at 350° for 45 minutes. Sprinkle with remaining 1 cup cheese; bake an additional 10 minutes. Yield: 12 servings.

CORN MUFFINS

1½ cups biscuit mix
½ cup cornmeal
2 tablespoons sugar
2 large eggs, beaten
⅔ cup milk

Combine first 3 ingredients in a large bowl; make a well in center of mixture. Combine eggs and milk; add to dry ingredients, stirring just until moistened. Spoon into greased muffin pans. Bake at 400° for 20 minutes or until golden brown. Yield: about 1 dozen.

NANNIE'S BISCUITS

⅔ cup shortening
1½ cups self-rising flour
⅔ cup buttermilk

Cut shortening into flour with a pastry blender until mixture resembles coarse meal. Add buttermilk, stirring with a fork until dry ingredients are moistened.

Turn dough out onto a floured surface; knead 4 or 5 times.

Roll dough out to ½-inch thickness, and cut with a 1½-inch biscuit cutter. Place biscuits on a lightly greased baking sheet; bake at 425° for 12 minutes or until golden brown. Yield: 3½ dozen.

GRILLED GARLIC BREAD

1 tablespoon plus 1½ teaspoons butter or
   margarine, softened
½ teaspoon garlic powder
½ (8-ounce) loaf French bread

Combine butter and garlic powder, stirring until blended. Cut French bread into 8 slices; spread each slice with butter mixture.

Grill French bread slices over medium coals 2 minutes. Turn bread slices, using hot pads or tongs, and grill an additional 2 minutes. Serve hot. Yield: 4 servings.

EASY GARLIC ROLLS

1 (1-pound) loaf frozen commercial bread
   dough, thawed
¼ cup butter or margarine, melted
1 large egg, beaten
1 tablespoon chopped fresh parsley
½ teaspoon garlic salt

Divide dough into 20 portions; shape each portion into a ball. Combine remaining ingredients, stirring well.

Dip dough balls into butter mixture; place in a greased 9-inch round cakepan. Cover and let rise in a warm place (85°), free from drafts, 1 hour or until doubled in bulk. Bake at 350° for 25 to 30 minutes or until golden. Yield: 20 rolls.

DESSERTS

BRANDY-CHOCOLATE MOUSSE

1 (6-ounce) package semisweet chocolate
   morsels
¼ cup plus 1 tablespoon butter or
   margarine
4 egg yolks, beaten
2 tablespoons brandy
¼ cup sifted powdered sugar
1 cup whipping cream, whipped
Garnish: sweetened whipped cream

Combine chocolate morsels and butter in
top of a double boiler; bring water to a boil.
Reduce heat to low; cook until chocolate and
butter melt.

Gradually stir about one-fourth of chocolate mixture into egg yolks; add to remaining
chocolate mixture, stirring constantly. Cook,
stirring constantly, 6 to 8 minutes or until
mixture reaches 160°. Remove from heat. Let
cool completely. Add brandy and powdered
sugar; stir well.

Fold whipped cream into chocolate mixture. Spoon mousse into individual serving
dishes; cover and chill until set. Garnish, if
desired. Yield: 6 servings.

BAKED CUSTARD

1½ cups milk
2 large eggs, beaten
2 tablespoons sugar
⅛ teaspoon salt
Dash of ground nutmeg
1 teaspoon vanilla extract
Sliced fresh strawberries
Fresh blueberries

Heat milk in a small saucepan to 120° to
130°. Combine eggs and next 4 ingredients;
stir until blended. Gradually add milk; stir
constantly. Pour mixture into four 6-ounce
custard cups. Set custard cups in a 9-inch
square baking pan; pour hot water into pan
to a depth of 1 inch.

Bake at 350° for 30 minutes or until a knife
inserted in center comes out clean. Remove
custard cups from water; cool. Refrigerate
until chilled. Top with fresh fruit before serving. Yield: 4 servings.

CHERRY CORDIAL DESSERT

½ gallon vanilla ice cream, softened
4 (1.45-ounce) milk chocolate candy bars,
   finely chopped
1 cup maraschino cherries, halved
½ cup coarsely chopped pecans
Sweetened whipped cream
Grated semisweet chocolate
Maraschino cherries
¼ cup crème de cacao, divided

Gently combine first 4 ingredients; spoon
into a 9-inch springform pan. Cover and
freeze until firm.

Place dessert on a serving platter, and remove rim from springform pan. Garnish with
whipped cream, grated chocolate, and
maraschino cherries. To serve, spoon about
1 teaspoon crème de cacao over each slice.
Serve immediately. Yield: one 9-inch dessert.

DELUXE BLUEBERRY CHEESECAKE

1½ cups graham cracker crumbs
2 tablespoons sugar
¼ cup plus 2 tablespoons butter or
   margarine, melted
1½ teaspoons ground cinnamon
3 (8-ounce) packages cream cheese,
   softened
1 cup sugar
3 large eggs
1 teaspoon vanilla extract, divided
1 (16-ounce) carton sour cream
3 tablespoons sugar
1 (21-ounce) can blueberry pie filling

Combine first 4 ingredients in a medium bowl; mix well. Press into a 10-inch spring-form pan; set aside.

Beat cream cheese in a large bowl until light. Gradually add 1 cup sugar, beating until fluffy. Add eggs, one at a time, beating well after each addition. Stir in ½ teaspoon vanilla. Pour cream cheese mixture into prepared pan; bake at 375° for 25 to 35 minutes or until cheesecake is set.

Beat sour cream in a small bowl at medium speed of an electric mixer for 2 minutes. Add 3 tablespoons sugar and remaining ½ teaspoon vanilla; beat 1 minute. Spread over cheesecake.

Bake cheesecake at 500° for 5 to 8 minutes or until bubbly. Remove from oven, and cool. Gently spread pie filling over top. Cover and refrigerate 8 hours. Place cheesecake on a serving platter, and remove rim from spring-form pan before serving. Yield: 10 servings.

CREAM CHEESE POUND CAKE

1½ cups chopped pecans, divided
1½ cups butter or margarine, softened
1 (8-ounce) package cream cheese, softened
3 cups sugar
6 large eggs
3 cups sifted cake flour
Dash of salt
1½ teaspoons vanilla extract

Sprinkle ½ cup pecans in a greased and floured 10-inch tube pan. Set aside.

Beat butter and cream cheese in a large bowl at medium speed of an electric mixer about 2 minutes or until soft and creamy. Gradually add sugar, beating at medium speed 5 to 7 minutes. Add eggs, one at a time, beating well after each addition. Add flour and salt, stirring until combined. Stir in vanilla and remaining 1 cup pecans. Pour batter into prepared pan.

Bake at 325° for 1½ hours or until a wooden pick inserted in center comes out clean. Cool in pan 10 minutes; remove from pan, and cool completely on a wire rack. Yield: one 10-inch cake.

COTTONWOOD CARROT CAKE

2 cups sifted cake flour
2 teaspoons baking soda
2 teaspoons ground cinnamon
2 teaspoons ground allspice
½ teaspoon salt
1⅓ cups vegetable oil
4 large eggs
2 cups sugar
3 cups grated carrots
Frosting

Combine first 5 ingredients, stirring well. Set dry ingredients aside.

Combine oil, eggs, and sugar in a large bowl; beat at medium speed of an electric mixer until blended. Add dry ingredients, beating well. Stir in carrots.

Pour batter into a greased and floured 13-x 9- x 2-inch baking pan. Bake at 325° for 55 minutes or until a wooden pick inserted in center comes out clean. Cool completely, and spread frosting over top of cake. Yield: one 13- x 9-inch cake.

Frosting:
1 (8-ounce) package cream cheese, softened
½ cup butter or margarine, softened
1 (16-ounce) package powdered sugar, sifted
½ cup raisins, chopped
½ cup flaked coconut
½ cup chopped pecans
1 teaspoon vanilla extract

Combine cream cheese and butter in a medium bowl; beat well at high speed of an electric mixer. Gradually add sugar; beat well. Add raisins and remaining ingredients; beat at high speed until frosting is spreading consistency. Yield: frosting for one 13- x 9-inch cake.

CHOCOLATE FUDGE CAKE

½ cup butter or margarine, softened
1 (16-ounce) package brown sugar
3 large eggs
3 (1-ounce) squares unsweetened
   chocolate, melted and cooled
2¼ cups sifted cake flour
2 teaspoons baking soda
½ teaspoon salt
1 (8-ounce) carton sour cream
1 cup hot water
1½ teaspoons vanilla extract
Frosting
Garnish: toasted pecan halves

Beat butter; gradually add brown sugar, beating well. Add eggs, one at a time, beating well after each addition. Add chocolate, mixing well.

Combine flour, soda, and salt; gradually add to chocolate mixture alternately with sour cream; beat well after each addition. Add water and vanilla; stir well.

Pour batter into 3 greased and floured 9-inch cakepans. Bake at 350° for 25 minutes or until a wooden pick inserted in center comes out clean. Let cool in pans 10 minutes. Remove from pans; place on wire racks to cool completely.

Spread frosting between layers and on top and sides of cake. Garnish top of cake, if desired. Yield: one 9-inch layer cake.

Frosting:

4 (1-ounce) squares unsweetened
   chocolate
⅓ cup butter or margarine
1 (16-ounce) package powdered
   sugar
½ cup milk
2 teaspoons vanilla extract

Combine chocolate and butter in a large saucepan; cook over low heat until melted, stirring constantly. Remove chocolate mixture from heat, and cool.

Sift powdered sugar; add to cooled chocolate mixture alternately with milk and vanilla. Beat at high speed of an electric mixer until spreading consistency. Yield: frosting for one 9-inch layer cake.

CRÈME DE MENTHE BROWNIES

½ cup butter or margarine, softened
1 cup sugar
4 large eggs
1 cup all-purpose flour
½ teaspoon salt
1 (16-ounce) can chocolate syrup
1 teaspoon vanilla extract
¼ cup butter or margarine, softened
2 cups sifted powdered sugar
2 tablespoons crème de menthe
1 (6-ounce) package semisweet chocolate
   morsels
¼ cup butter or margarine

Beat ½ cup butter in a medium bowl; gradually add 1 cup sugar, beating until light and fluffy. Add eggs, one at a time, beating well after each addition.

Combine flour and salt; add to creamed mixture alternately with chocolate syrup, beginning and ending with flour mixture. Stir in vanilla.

Pour batter into a greased and floured 13- x 9- x 2-inch baking pan. Bake at 350° for 25 to 30 minutes. Cool completely (brownies will shrink from sides of pan while cooling).

Beat ¼ cup butter in a medium mixing bowl; gradually add 2 cups powdered sugar and crème de menthe, mixing well. Spread mixture evenly over brownies; cover and chill about 1 hour.

Combine morsels and ¼ cup butter in top of a double boiler; bring water to a boil. Reduce heat to low; cook until chocolate and butter melt. Spread over brownies; cover and chill at least 1 hour. Cut into squares. Yield: 3½ dozen.

S'MORES

6 (1.45-ounce) milk chocolate candy bars,
   broken in half crosswise
12 graham crackers, broken in half
   crosswise
12 large marshmallows

Place candy bar halves on top of 12 graham cracker halves. Toast marshmallows over an open fire. Place toasted marshmallows on top of chocolate, and cover with remaining graham cracker halves to form a sandwich. Press to seal. Serve immediately. Yield: 12 servings.

LEMON MERINGUE PIE

1½ cups sugar
⅓ cup cornstarch
¼ teaspoon salt
1½ cups cold water
½ cup lemon juice
5 large eggs, separated
2 tablespoons butter or margarine
1 to 2 teaspoons grated lemon rind
1 baked 9-inch pastry shell
¼ teaspoon cream of tartar
½ cup plus 2 tablespoons sugar
½ teaspoon vanilla extract

Combine first 3 ingredients in a large saucepan, stirring well. Gradually add water and lemon juice, stirring until smooth.

Beat egg yolks until thick and pale; gradually stir into lemon mixture. Add butter. Cook over medium heat, stirring constantly, until thickened and bubbly. Cook mixture an additional minute, stirring constantly. Remove from heat, and stir in grated lemon rind. Pour into prepared pastry shell.

Combine egg whites and cream of tartar in a large bowl; beat until foamy. Gradually add ½ cup plus 2 tablespoons sugar, 1 tablespoon at a time, beating until stiff peaks form. Add vanilla. Spread meringue over filling, sealing to edge of pastry. Bake at 325° for 25 minutes or until meringue is brown. Cool completely. Yield: one 9-inch pie.

OLD-FASHIONED PEACH COBBLER

4 cups sliced fresh peaches
1 cup sugar
½ cup butter or margarine
1½ cups all-purpose flour
¾ teaspoon salt
½ cup shortening
¼ cup plus 1 tablespoon cold water

Combine sliced peaches, sugar, and butter in a medium saucepan; bring to a boil. Reduce heat, and simmer, uncovered, until peaches are tender and mixture thickens. Pour peach mixture into a lightly buttered 10- x 6- x 2-inch baking dish, and set aside.

Combine flour and salt in a small bowl; cut in shortening with a pastry blender until mixture resembles coarse meal. Sprinkle water evenly over flour mixture, and stir with a fork until all ingredients are moistened. Shape pastry into a ball.

Roll pastry out to ⅛-inch thickness on a lightly floured surface; cut into 1-inch strips. Arrange half of strips in lattice design over peaches. Bake at 350° for 35 minutes. Remove from oven, and gently press baked pastry into peach mixture. Repeat lattice design over peaches with remaining pastry strips. Return cobbler to oven, and bake an additional 40 minutes. Yield: 6 servings.

CINNAMON-BAKED APPLES

6 large baking apples, peeled and cored
¼ cup plus 2 tablespoons sugar, divided
1½ teaspoons ground cinnamon, divided
1½ teaspoons ground nutmeg, divided
2 tablespoons butter or margarine, divided
½ to ¾ cup apple juice
Red food coloring (optional)

Place apples in a 2-quart casserole; spoon 1 tablespoon sugar into each apple. Sprinkle each with ¼ teaspoon cinnamon and ¼ teaspoon nutmeg; top with 1 teaspoon butter.

Place apple juice in a saucepan, and bring to a boil; stir in food coloring, if desired. Pour mixture into casserole. Bake, uncovered, at 400° for 50 to 60 minutes or until tender; baste occasionally with juice mixture. Yield: 6 servings.

MENUS

PICNIC ON THE GROUNDS
(serves 8)
Mediterranean Spring Salad (page 47)
Picnic Barbecued Chicken (page 39)
Corn-on-the-Cob with
Herb Butter (page 50)
Commercial Italian Bread
Chocolate Fudge Cake (page 56)

BEEF 'N' BISCUITS
(serves 6)
German Potato Salad (page 49)
Barbecued Chuck Roast (page 10)
Fresh Broccoli Spears
Nannie's Biscuits (page 53)
Vanilla Ice Cream with Fresh Strawberries

MEET ME AT GRANDMA'S
(serves 6)
Marinated Tomato Slices (page 47)
Country-Style Ribs (page 32)
Herb-Seasoned Green Beans (page 50)
Corn Pudding (page 51)
Cream Cheese Pound Cake (page 55)

KABOBS FOR FOUR
(serves 4)
Mixed Fresh Fruit Salad
Shish Kabobs Teriyaki (page 25)
Hot Cooked Yellow Rice
Buttered Peas
Cherry Cordial Dessert (page 54)

SOUTHWESTERN CAMPFIRE
(serves 12)
Crispy Coleslaw (page 48)
Grilled Brisket with
Panhandle Barbecue Sauce (page 11)
Fresh Lima Beans
Mexican Cornbread (page 53)
Cottonwood Carrot Cake (page 55)

SUPPER PARTY FOR TEENS
(serves 12)
Country-Style Coleslaw (page 48)
Frankfurters with Condiments (page 16)
Potato Chips
S'mores (page 56)

A MENU MOSTLY GRILLED
(serves 4)
Tossed Green Salad
Honey-Glazed Chicken (page 39)
Vegetables in a Packet (page 52)
Grilled Garlic Bread (page 53)
Baked Custard (page 54)

SUNDAY DINNER FAVORITES
(serves 6)
Simply Good Salad (page 47)
Marinated Pork Tenderloins (page 29)
Charcoal-Baked Potatoes (page 51)
Fresh Green Beans
Easy Garlic Rolls (page 53)
Old-Fashioned Peach Cobbler (page 57)

SPECIAL FOR COMPANY
(serves 6)
Boston Tossed Salad (page 48)
Grilled Lobster Tails (page 21)
Zippy Zucchini Skillet (page 52)
Assorted Hard Rolls
Brandy-Chocolate Mousse (page 54)

GRILLING FOR GUESTS THE FANCY WAY
(serves 10)
Lemon-Barbecued Turkey (page 35)
Hot Cooked Rice
Steamed Asparagus
Commercial Rolls
Deluxe Blueberry Cheesecake *(page 54)*

CROWD-PLEASIN' COOKOUT
(serves 8)
Tossed Green Salad
Stuffed Hamburgers (page 16)
Baked Beans
Sour Cream Potato Salad (page 49)
Crème de Menthe Brownies (page 56)

SPRINGTIME FARE
(serves 4)
Spinach Salad (page 48)
Lamb Chops with Béarnaise Sauce (page 24)
Parsley New Potatoes (page 51)
Summer Garden Medley (page 52)
Lemon Meringue Pie (page 57)

EASY MIDWEEK DINNER
(serves 6)
Tossed Green Salad
Grilled Grouper (page 18)
Easy Succotash (page 52)
Commercial Rolls
Cinnamon-Baked Apples (page 57)

A MEAT AND POTATOES SUPPER
(serves 6)
Seven-Layer Salad (page 47)
Grilled Black Pepper Steak (page 13)
Herbed Potatoes on the Grill (page 51)
Cheesy Stuffed Squash (page 52)
Corn Muffins (page 53)
Orange Sherbet

INDEX